Staying Calm in the Midst of Chaos™

Staying Calm in the Midst of Chaos™

How to Keep Positive in an Unsettled World

Carolyn Gross

Creative Living Publications
ESCONDIDO, CALIFORNIA

First printing 2002

ISBN 0-9718064-0-3

LCCN 2002102140

ATTENTION CORPORATIONS, UNIVERSITIES, COLLEGES, AND PROFESSIONAL ORGANIZATIONS: Quantity discounts are available on bulk purchases of this book for educational, gift purposes, or as premiums for increasing magazine subscriptions or renewals. Special books or book excerpts can also be created to fit specific needs. For information, please contact Creative Living Publications, 306 NW El Norte Parkway, Suite 426, Escondido, CA 92026; ph. 760-741-2762.

Dedicated to You

If you blame yourself for the pain you have suffered,
I believe this…

"If there is a wound
We must try to heal it.
If there is someone whose pain we can cure
We must search till we find them.
If the Gods have chosen that we should survive
It will be for a reason."

—EXCERPT FROM THE MOVIE
CAPTAIN CORELLI'S MANDOLIN

Namaste

ACKNOWLEDGMENTS

My highest praise and appreciation goes to my husband Bryan, who has the patience of Job. Thank you for coming into my life at the perfect time and for growing with me. You are my calm in chaos.

For all the fun things we do, thanks Mom for: teaching, loving, and supporting me to realize my dreams. You don't waste a day!

Heartfelt thanks to Beverly Trainer for her editorial services and being the midwife for this creative process.

For proofing and editing support, thank you Aleta Pippin, you're a stellar artist and friend.

Resonating with this book, I thank you, Kate Deubert, for the polishing and proofing. An asset to writers everywhere...special thanks to Marilyn and Tom Ross at About Books, Inc., and Cathy Bowman for outstanding book design. Marilyn, you are a true publishing Goddess!

My supportive teachers in my own healing journey: Ken Sutherland, Judith Larkin Reno, Sandra Lee, Joy Day, Carolyn Mein, Phyllis Light, Mark Haskins, and Roberta Zito.

For all my wonderful clients who trusted me with their healing journeys and made my own life richer, you know who you are!

For blessing me with your long-term friendship: Lorraine Saunders, Joy Childers, Valarie McClure, Judi Menzel, Jan DeLeon, and Bonnie Trescott—each of you showing me that love truly is the greatest gift of all.

Special thanks for your input on this project: Nicole Mignon, Monica Montgomery, Ray Payn, Rodger Price, Francine Schneider, and Phyllis Light.

To the National Speakers Association—What an organization—for helping make dreams come true for someone like me! My deepest admiration and appreciation to those who help light my fire and show me the way: Barbara Sanfilippo, Tom Bay, Mary-Ellen Drummond, Jim Cathcart, Greg Godek, Janet Lapp, Brian Tracy, Mark LeBlanc, Marcia Steele, Jeff Salz, Arden and Carolyn Bercovitz, Sarita Maybin, Nanci McGraw, Rob Sommer, Ben Kubassek, Joni Wilson, Warren and Brenda Woods.

TABLE OF CONTENTS

CHAPTER ONE

Chaos:
The Great Teacher

"There is more to life than increasing its speed."

—GANDHI

No matter how confident some people may appear, no one just breezes through life. There are times when we all become overwhelmed, make mistakes, fall down. Overextended, overtired, understaffed…these words all conjure up images of chaos. As members of the most privileged and advanced society ever to exist, we find ourselves facing epic levels of stress.

Stress is not a middle-of-the-road situation. It lives in the fringes, but permeates every aspect of our lives. No one wants to be overworked and underpaid, or forced to juggle enough responsibility for three people. Yet these situations are commonplace and we rarely learn how to handle the resulting stress until we're desperate.

For many of us, it's a personal or health-related crisis that finally forces the issue. Heart attack survivors are classic examples of those who make lifestyle changes under duress. Many experts speculate that up to 80 percent of all illnesses are stress related. And no wonder. The miracles of technology have forced us to become multi-taskers and multi–role players. Instead of saving us precious time, the high tech world adds labor to our lives. We may no longer lick stamps and address envelopes, but now we must respond to e-mails, and answer pagers and cell phones around the clock as we try to keep up with the information overload. We sometimes get results by flipping a switch, but we must also contend with computers that crash and equipment that diabolically goes on the blink at the worst possible time.

Pain: When Is It a Warning?

Even those who think they aren't achieve-aholics often take dreams of peace to their graves—or to the hospital—because they never made time for serenity during their vital years. One of my clients, a high-profile beauty salon owner, was working 12-hour days in her shop while saddled with administrative duties. She came to me complaining of neck pain so intense she couldn't turn her head. "My neck hurts all the time," she explained. "I work on people's heads all day and now my own head is killing me. Can you do anything?"

Having worked as a stress consultant and CranioSacral therapist for 12 years, I was able to answer yes. The effects of constant chaos are very physical. During times of stress the sympathetic nervous system prevails. That means the heart rate rises, vessels widen to increase blood flow, glucose levels are elevated, saliva and gastric acid production diminish, gastrointestinal activity ceases, and skeletal muscle strength intensifies. Translated: our heart races, digestion ceases, adrenaline secretion is high, and the body is ready for action.

During rest, the parasympathetic system dominates as we rebuild and release. The heart rate decreases, digestive processes are stimulated, and gastrointestinal elimination is activated. This is where life balance happens.

As a result of nerve activity, tensions resulting from chaos are frequently stored in the core of the body: the head, neck, and spine. In the practice of CranioSacral therapy, those are the areas we address, for they activate the parasympathetic nervous system. The gentle manipulations during treatment allow stored tensions to unwind. As this pressure is released, the body begins to heal and balance itself.

After years of interviewing clients prior to treatment, I found a striking correlation between mind and body functions. Shoulder pain, for example, often occurs when people take on too much responsibility. Back ailments are common for those who lack support or feel financially insecure. For my hairdresser client, her pace of life was literally a pain in the neck. She was so focused on being a successful business owner that she ignored her body's cry for help. During her consultation I urged her to slow down. "You clearly need more time off," I counseled. "I can get your neck in great shape in a few sessions, but if you don't make some changes, you'll be wasting your money."

Pain is a great motivator, and my client desperately wanted to feel better. She began by cutting back her hours and hiring an additional stylist. The salon still netted the same money and she now felt happier and healthier. I can't tell you how many people I've worked with who found that when they reduced their work hours and increased their exercise, relaxation, bodywork, hobbies, and leisure time, they still managed to maintain their income while upgrading their lifestyle. Trust me, it can be done!

When we allow time for the parasympathetic system to restore us we have more clarity. According to Brian Tracy, one of the great authors and educators of today, 80 percent of goal achievement is the result of clarity.

What Price Success?

When the vast majority of people experience a near-fatal illness or accident, they rarely regret the unreturned phone call or an uncompleted sales report. Instead they lament time not spent with loved ones, cancelled vacations, and unfulfilled passions.

This principle calls to mind a successful real estate mogul who was hell-bent on making his first million by age 30. Pushing himself to the limit, he managed to fulfill his boyhood dream. After three decades he had it all: money, power, a lovely wife, and four children. And then he collapsed. His breakdown was so severe that he was unable to return to work for two years. Bedridden with depression, he had plenty of time to reflect on the high cost of his Trump-like fantasies. In time he was able to parlay his story into a book, and he began speaking to audiences on How to Succeed Without Burnout. Ben

Kubassek eventually returned to work and today his life is prospering. He's happy and fulfilled, *and* he has learned the invaluable lesson of working without pushing over the precipice into chaos. Why is managing chaos and stress such a hot topic today? Because most of us need permission to slow down and really pay attention to our own needs. Many of us push ourselves into 60-hour work weeks while raising our families, taking classes, keeping fit, trying to look young, and winning the occasional award. We go, go, go......but do we know where we are going? Someone once said, "If life is a race, then the finish line is the graveyard."

One of the chief indicators of chaos is a body that feels out of alignment. When we go into crisis mode, the body's homeostasis is thrown off balance. This may manifest itself in the form of neck pain, headaches, digestive problems, chronic back or shoulder aches, fatigue or depression. And a body chronically out of balance will eventually succumb to heart disease, cancer, high blood pressure, obesity, and digestive problems.

We cannot control 100 percent of the events in our lives, but we can control our reactions to them. We cannot guarantee that our loved ones—or we ourselves—will always be healthy, nor can we predict our financial future or job success. But no matter what curveballs knock us for a loop, we *can* master our response to these events. To me the only safety net we truly have is how we act and react to what life serves up.

This is how chaos becomes the great teacher—we learn in the midst of a crisis just how strong we really are. Sometimes we find more inner resources than we give ourselves credit for; other times we discover our vulnerabilities. Often when we embark on a new enterprise—a business, a relationship, a creative project—we find surprising reserves of energy and enthusiasm that enable us to achieve that first heady feeling of success.

Then one day we wake up and feel less passion and drive. We may notice that we're relying on unhealthy lifestyle choices to sustain us—too many lattes and hi-cal snacks by day and more than a social drink to unwind at night. We can get away with these habits for a while, but eventually these crutches will age us before our time. The minute we realize we're using quick fixes (Starbucks, anyone?) just to get through our daily routine, it's time to reevaluate and catch up with ourselves.

I once heard about an actress who simultaneously starred in a hit TV series by day and had the leading role in a Broadway play at night. It seemed a nearly superhuman feat. *What a woman!* But on a television talk show she confessed that she had become a caffeine junkie, downing seven or eight cups of coffee a day. I couldn't help thinking, *What a role model for unhealthy living!* I haven't heard much about her lately, but I do hope she's managed to survive. Caffeine and chaos go together. Neither allows the parasympathetic activity the time it needs to rebuild and rest.

When I present seminars and workshops, I take people through an exercise where they review a list of stress symptoms. If someone has two or three symptoms, I inform them they are in the right room and need to pay attention to the program. It is not uncommon for people to report as many as eight or ten symptoms of stress out of a possible fourteen. This to me is a clear indicator of a health problem waiting to happen.

The way to give yourself permission to make changes is to value your health and your heart enough to make lifestyle adjustments before stress evolves into serious illness. The purpose of this book is to offer you tools to help you stay calm and prioritize your life. Once armored with these techniques, you can enter the chaos of our fast-paced society, achieve success, and make a contribution to the world without sacrificing your own life and health.

CHAPTER TWO

Trusting the Life Process

"In a dark time the mind begins to see."
—THEODORE ROETHKE

I was driving down California's Golden State Freeway after a long Thanksgiving weekend, the traffic heavy in all eight lanes. I'd left Orange County on an emotional edge, and my tension was mounting with every lane change. After spending four days with my fiancé and his surrogate family, I was starting to realize this man and his life were not right for me. I hadn't yet told him what I was feeling because I was still trying to sort things out.

After traveling south about 10 miles I realized I was flirting with a speeding ticket, so I cruised into the slow lane, something I rarely do. After a few snail-paced miles, a car entering the freeway suddenly sideswiped my right rear fender, sending me into a spin. I never saw him coming and suddenly I was in a crisis. The sensation of slow motion started as I tried to get the car under control, and the next thing I knew I was hurtling off the side of the road. That's when an aura of light flooded the car and surrounded me as my vehicle rolled over and cascaded down a steep ravine. When the car finally crash-landed, it was in an upside-down position, and I was right side up.

While my life and body were spinning out of control, I continued to be immersed in the aura of light and almost seemed to float down the hillside. But when I tried to move and get out of the car, the door wouldn't open. In a panic, I managed to squeeze out the window, then crawl out into the brush where I finally struggled to my feet. I looked up to see a tall man on the shoulder above me, asking if I was okay. "I called an ambulance and they're on the way!" he hollered down.

I smiled and waved, knowing already what the doctors would later confirm. I had somehow escaped with nothing more than a few bruises.

I'd been the recipient of a gift, a definite miracle.

* * * *

How do you react when life throws a catastrophe your way? Disaster comes in many forms: an accident, the loss of a job, a scam that wipes out your retirement fund, a family member who becomes a criminal, a sudden disability or life-threatening illness, the loss of one's home. Do you immediately respond, "Thank you, God, this must be a blessing in disguise"? Or do you tense up and think *Oh my God, what next*? Before my accident—which I prefer to call an "incident"—I used to take even minor incidents quite personally, and I definitely didn't roll with the punches. If I lost a job or didn't close a sale, if I received a

Dear Jane letter or failed to get recognition for my work, I took it all to heart.

What I've learned since my *incident* is that I can create inner chaos—or not—simply by the way I react to life events. As advocates of positive thinking have been saying for years, "It's not what happens to us that matters—it's how we respond."

My reactions to life events used to be out of balance. I'd overreact to certain situations or shrug off others with too much denial. One early denial experience took place when I was laid off from a job for which I had uprooted my life and moved halfway across the country. When the company had to cut back on labor, they let five managers go in one day. Instead of crying or getting upset I said to myself, "It doesn't matter." And without much angst, I moved to San Diego with my best friend. But for over a year I had nightmares about this job; it was the only way I could deal with my loss. I had given my heart and soul to my employer and *POW!*—the end came brutally and without warning.

Another time in my youth, I was involved with a less-than-monogamous Italian playboy. When I discovered the extent of his escapades, I'd go on and on about how badly he was treating me, instead of ending the relationship and getting on with my life. This pattern of talking incessantly about self-created problems and taxing my friends with my latest soap opera lasted years too long.

Demon in a Glass

It was during this time I had to face the fact that I could not consume alcohol in moderation. Once I drank that first beer or glass of wine, I wanted more. And more. This was difficult because I'd been raised in a family of social drinkers who were productive in life and able to enjoy nightly cocktails without problems. Not me. One drink always turned into many. By the time I was in my late twenties I could no longer tell myself, "I can drink less any time I want to." I knew I had to stop.

Being in sales didn't make it easy. I'd go to meetings and trade shows where my colleagues ended their day at the hotel happy hour. I knew if I tried to join them I'd soon be tempted to replace my Perrier with some liquid happiness. So I'd go out to dinner alone and wind up in front of the television, separating myself from the crew, because it was the only way I could keep sober.

I eventually found help by surrendering to a lifestyle equipped with a higher power and support groups. As I entered into this new way of life, I soon realized I'd have to keep my distance from situations that threatened my healthy commitments.

One of my early trials-by-fire took place at the wedding of an old college friend in Colorado. I had recently been promoted to district sales manager, and that state was part of my territory, so I conveniently scheduled a trip to Denver a few days before the wedding.

As soon as I arrived I began to feel sick. I made it through my two workdays, doing everything I could think of to boost my energy and feel better. On Friday a group of old college friends were going to get together to reminisce.

The day felt unbearable the moment I awoke. My first thought was *I'd better not push myself.* Even though I'd bought a new dress, purchased an expensive gift, and was ready to see my old pals, I called one trusted friend and told her of my trepidations. I mentioned I was sober and her words were less than encouraging. "Well," she said, "there'll be a lot of partying this weekend, you can bet on it." *Bingo!* I knew I had to cancel. The moment I announced I wasn't feeling well and would have to take a raincheck, I hung up the phone and miraculously felt well again for the first time in days.

I know beyond a doubt that had I attended this event I would have given up my commitment to an alcohol-free life. Many times throughout the years my body has issued these warning signs when I'm headed for trouble. After having several such experiences, I began to trust the process of my life and learned how to listen to my body and inner promptings.

If something feels unbearable—it probably is. There is nothing wrong with you if you decide it's in your best interest to decline an invitation, even at the last minute. This to me is the ultimate trusting process. We often feel so committed once we have accepted an invitation or position, we think we no longer have a choice. But we do have a choice, and knowing that gives us power. When inner anxiety tells me something will drain, deplete, or divert me from my goals, then I gracefully bow out. Listening to my body is a critical component on how I make decisions. Years of self-healing and alternative healing have given me access so I can hear my body's wisdom. Life is the great teacher; I've learned that the greatest obstacle one has to overcome will likely become the greatest blessing.

Some "Drugs" Come Candy-Wrapped

My father's side of the family tended toward obesity. When I was growing up people commented on my appetite for sweets and also on my cooking skills. I clearly had my dad's genes when it came to food. But early on I knew I wanted to avoid looking like my 200-pound aunt or 300-pound grandmother. My fear of becoming obese became a driving force in my life. Just as with alcohol, I knew I had to do something about my eating habits, because I kept gaining and losing the same 30+ pounds over and over. My weakness was sweets; candy and desserts were an escape from life's problems and disappointments.

In an attempt to find a solution to my weight problem, I considered a food plan that had no sugar, wheat, or flour. Had I heard about this at any other time I might not have given it a second thought. But I was eight years sober and food had become my new drug. I'd go on eating binges and at the same time obsess over trying to stay thin.

It was a month of popcorn, flavored coffees, and sugar-free frozen yogurt that left me feeling crazy. In the midst of this binge I was very angry with God. I yelled and screamed at Him or Her that I had changed my life so completely for the good, yet here I was a bleeping mess. As the Apostle Paul once wrote, "You are never closer to God than when you are angry with Him." It was during this rage that I heard about a book that would change my life. *Food Addiction—The Body Knows* by Kay Sheppard introduced me to the idea of abstaining from sugar, just as I did with alcohol. The book mentioned that wheat and flour might be a problem as well, and it suggested eliminating these three items entirely.

That was easier said than done. In my wildest dreams I never imagined having to relinquish all the foods that contain these ingredients in order to stabilize my body, mind, and spirit. But for me, that turned out to be the solution. For the first time in my life my body weight stabilized. No longer did I have to fear the scale galloping toward the 200 mark; nor did I have to worry about regaining those on-and-off-again 30 pounds.

As soon as I committed to a healthier diet and began living on a higher plane, I found myself tested once again. Did I mention my career? I worked in the food industry for 20 years and spent the latter years as a food broker in sales and marketing. My clients were high quality manufacturers. After I began abstaining from sugar, wheat, and flour, I continued to sell these foods, but I could no longer eat them.

I did my job well. My boss was so pleased with my performance that he wanted to show his appreciation. M&M's/Mars were part of the Uncle Ben's conglomerate, and as a reward for doing a good job, Uncle Ben's gave us a new line to represent, Ethel M Chocolates. This is a gourmet line of confections made in Las Vegas, spun-off from the M&M's/Mars fortune. Ethel was the mother of the clan; hence Ethel M Chocolates became the new kid on the upscale candy block. My boss said, "Carolyn, I'd like you to be the account manager for Ethel M. Congratulations!"

So there I was, nine months off all forms of sugar, and I was about to represent a world-class chocolate line. Within days Federal Express delivered two large boxes filled with 40 pounds of mouthwatering samples to get me acquainted with the product. Resisting occasional temptation is one thing, but living on an intimate basis with thought-I'd-died-and-gone-to-heaven–caliber truffles is something else. I panicked. How could I not succumb to temptation? Where could I possibly hide these seductive morsels so they'd be out of sight *and* out of mind? As dragon-sized doubts raced through my brain, I opened the front hall closet, placed all 40 pounds of chocolate inside, and slammed the door.

Then I sat in my living room wondering *Where am I going to get the strength to open these boxes and not eat myself silly?* Suddenly I had a vision of my 300-pound grandmother. I began to recall a childhood memory, when she would tell us, "If you want some goodies go to the front hall closet."

Grandmother had such a sweet tooth that she actually bribed the bakery men at her local grocery store. Entenmann's and Awrey's trucks would deliver to her home during their weekly runs because her high consumption made it worth their while. When the racks of goodies arrived, she had them stored in her front hall closet where she kept her stash. Strength somehow came to me through this recollection. *Don't let history repeat itself*, I told myself, over and over.

I never did sample a single chocolate during my tenure as a food broker, nor have I since. I don't take full credit for this, for I believe we are given strength in times like this by a greater power, the same power and light that entered my tumbling car that fateful Thanksgiving weekend.

When I look back on my life, I think it has this spiritual quality, as does everyone's if he or she will trust and seek the higher way. Throughout this journey of transformation, seminars, support groups, churches, and inspirational organizations provide a forum for encouragement and fellowship as we grow.

A Turn in the Road

Another part of the trusting process involves working with each avenue presented to me from the most spiritual to the most clinical. Guided by the "calling-card experiences" in my life, I would often hear about a particular class or teacher that coincided with my issues of focus at the time. I'd then proceed to take action. One thing led to the next and my life began to unfold in a new, almost effortless way. I trusted the serendipity of this food-addiction book coming my way when I was desperate to resolve my eating issues. That is how the trusting process begins.

Whenever I get out of control or off track, solutions I'd never dreamed of suddenly appear. My greatest struggles have resulted in my greatest periods of growth. *No pain, no gain.* Yet I always have to remember that *too much* pain is not a good thing. It's important to develop awareness about when to embrace the pain of facing shortcomings and when to let go of painful situations because the chaos would be destructive.

I developed my skills as a facilitator for healing under such conditions. I mentioned earlier my position as a food broker. I had worked in the field for nearly 15 years when I realized this job was not my passion nor where I wanted to spend my future. My soul had been gradually awakening as the result of my lifestyle changes. Most of my vacations were retreats to spiritual conventions or alone time in nature communing with God.

My food broker position afforded me the ability to purchase my first home. When I received my mortgage coupon book and began writing those four figure checks, I thought I'd never have money for another trip. Then I heard about a convention on the July 4th weekend, up the coast in Seattle. I really wanted to attend but didn't see how I could afford the airfare.

As I resigned myself to the likelihood I'd have to pass, a Delta Airlines rep called just before the convention and said, "We have your round-trip tickets to Seattle!" It was uncanny. Months earlier I had taken advantage of a promotional offer and had mailed in a grocery receipt along with the holiday weekend request, never expecting anything to come of it. And then, voilà! I was off to Seattle, credit card in hand.

After a couple days at the convention I felt like I wanted to get away from the downtown area and check out Mount Rainier National Park. I rented a car, unconcerned that it was a holiday weekend and I had no accommodations. When I arrived I just sat on the steps of this lovely lodge near the park entrance, gazing at majestic Mount Rainier. People have said that its beauty is often hidden by clouds, so I decided I would do well to soak in this glorious sight on a crystal-clear sunny day. I must have spent an hour just gazing at the blue skies and snow-covered mountain with 17 glaciers right before me. I was so mesmerized by this grandeur that I didn't want to go back to town, so I tried to find a room for the night. Everything was predictably sold out, but one clerk told me to come back around four o'clock to check on cancellations.

I noticed a trailhead across the street and decided I had time for a hike. It was called "The Trail of Shadows" because of the immense trees covering the path, producing ferns and moss and all the rich vegetation that grows in humid climates. There was a little loop trail where the founding pioneers had settled in an idyllic spot by the hot springs. The frame of a one-room cabin remained as proof that the settlers had really lived there and walked those trails.

I felt so inspired in that deep forest, almost catapulted into a different dimension. I sat by the cabin imagining the comings and goings of the early settlers. Suddenly my mind was flooded with a vision. Not wanting this experience to get away, I began to write in my journal. There amidst the trees, bathed in a golden glow, I realized that what I really wanted was to be a speaker, a teacher, a healer. I wanted to inspire and help people transform their lives. The vision continued and I could see myself somewhere in the years ahead, speaking and signing books, and feeling that all was well in my life. I literally traveled into the future that day and saw a new me.

By the time I left Mount Rainier (oh, yes, there was room at the inn for me that night), I felt energy coursing through my body that I'd never experienced before. I didn't sleep a wink. I wrote incessantly and walked the Trail of Shadows several more times. As life-altering a transition as it would be, I was determined to make this vision my goal—and my life. I knew I was embarking on a whole new path, a higher level of living. The date I noted in my journal was July 7, 1990, my own Independence Day.

Living the Dream—One Day at a Time

I spent the next six years working part-time, nights and evenings, doing CranioSacral therapy and healing my own life. The healing gifts in my hands had been there since childhood and I knew I had to incorporate them into my career. As I was moved on to advanced courses in healing, I was asked to instruct beginner classes. Hair salons would hire me to teach healing techniques and touch to their stylists. I was still working 40-hour weeks in the food industry, and I was working full-time to achieve my vision. It helped that during this time I happened to be single and living a monastic lifestyle. My personal life was on hold. All I cared about was learning how to help, to heal, and develop as a speaker.

During the next six years I wanted to quit my day job many times. The last year or so my ambitious schedule began to take its toll on my health. I began taking anywhere from three to nine ibuprofen just to get through a day of sales calls and meetings. I suffered from back pain and other ailments, and to add to my stress, the food cans I had stored in my garage started exploding for no apparent reason. I wanted out badly but I was waiting for some kind of sign to let me know it was the right time. Since the vision at Mount Rainier wasn't something I had planned or orchestrated, I figured that God would let me know when to make my big move.

During this time I was enrolled in an Artist's Way class and about halfway through the course I asked the instructor for a private meeting. I told him I was going to launch a career as a professional speaker and I explained that I'd been preparing for the past six years. His first question was, "When are you going to do this?" It was now July 1996. I figured by the end of the year—maybe. But this wise man said, "I don't think you're going to make it that long." I knew he might be right. The demands of my job had been increasing, but I was determined to stick it out a while longer and leave at a high point. I'd been with the company eight years and brought in lots of new business. Cutting those ties wouldn't be easy.

It happened that I had signed up for yet another seminar and had requested a few days off to attend. I thought, *This seminar will really get me ready to fly.* The day before I left for San Francisco I was so stressed that I had sneaked off to the beach to eat my lunch. While I sat there with my toes in the sand, I was paged three times in 30 minutes. No rest for the weary. But in spite of the interruptions, I was determined to get centered. So I lay down on a stretch of grass in search of a few moments of peace, in my three-piece business suit and all. It was then that my letter of resignation seemed to write itself in my overworked brain. At the end of the day I typed the exact words that had come to me at the beach and carefully penned in my signature.

By September of 1996, after a 20-year career, I left the food business for good. As I was in the process of launching my speaking business, one of my buddies who worked for the Marriott chain said to me, "Carolyn, come in and do a program for our staff on stress management." He gave me the choice of either late June or early July. I said, "What about July 7th, 1997?" Here I was, seven years later on the exact date of my Mount Rainier vision, starting to live my dream.

Stress Management Starts from Within

Now that I've told you my story, let's talk about ways to move our lives to a higher plane, a calmer way of living, so we can rise above the chaos. For me it always begins on a physical level, because stress is such a physical thing. After burning out twice before the age of 40, I had to address my high-stress personality as I tried to cope with the problems of daily life. I stumbled into the healing arts in the process of healing my own life, and discovered a knack for connecting mental beliefs and emotional patterns with the physical symptoms of disease. This led to a career as a CranioSacral therapist and professional speaker. Today I know beyond any doubt that the solutions to stress reside within the body's own intelligence—if we will only listen.

This book does not diagnose stress symptoms, which over time become chronic illness. Rather it introduces ways of slowing down to heal the emotional patterns and belief systems that create stress and disease. There are many types of physical treatments, both traditional and alternative.

The stories I tell of my life are to help you identify some of your own beliefs, patterns, and motives that create stress. You can change these stressful ways and increase awareness and life potential. I promise you this will happen as you learn to trust the process of your life.

CHAPTER THREE

Symptoms of Stress

"Stress can take natural abilities and drive, and destroy them. An over-stressed individual…may become irrational, procrastinate, put out sloppy work, miss time, experience more illness, and make wrong decisions…."

—B. J. RONE

We need to acquaint ourselves with the symptoms of stress for one very important reason—*prevention.* In the final five years of the 20th century, the cost of stress in the workplace virtually tripled. One study estimates a cost of up to $750 per employee annually, in terms of lost productivity and healthcare expenses. Managers should understand that if they don't mentor their staff in taking care of themselves, the bottom line will suffer.

If we pay attention to stress symptoms and stop popping antidepressants and/or stimulants, we can prevent illness and imbalances, as well as decreased job performance. I once had a boss who would take non-drowsy cold medication just for the energy boost. Can you relate? What is *your* quick fix when you feel depleted?

In his book *Spirituality, Stress, and You*, Baptist minister Thomas Rodgerson wrote that he once delivered a sermon at his new parish after staying up half the night to prepare. As the congregation greeted him after the service, a 97-year-old woman approached him, shook his hand, and said, "You're operating without any reserve of energy. Go home and take a nap before you wear your body out!" Astute lady that she was, she ministered to the minister that day.

How often do we ignore our bodies' messages in the form of headaches, fatigue, or flu because we—like that minister—think we must press on? Certainly there are times when we have no choice, when situations dictate extraordinary measures. One example is an executive who was interviewed on *60 Minutes*. He was doing damage control for his company under litigation by thousands worldwide, and hadn't had a day off for 10 weeks. The footage showed his two young sons playing at his office on a Sunday, just so they could be with their dad. A close-up of the executive revealed a shingles-like rash all over his face. He clearly looked a wreck. He was doing what he had to do, negotiating day and night—but the price was high.

The only way we can pull off this kind of feat is to have a reserve account of strength and energy. Whenever we allow the parasympathetic system time to rest and restore us, we are depositing energy to shore us up during times of crisis. Much like money in the bank, you add to this account when you sleep, eat healthy foods, receive massages, go on vacation, or do whatever it is that restores your soul. For some it might be hiking, golfing, reading, or even cooking. It doesn't matter what it is; it only matters that you make these lifesaving deposits. When you have a healthy balance in your "crisis reserve account," you're more able to handle job or relationship changes, illness, or other calamities. And when a crisis is over, your first priority might be to rebuild your reserves so you'll be ready for the next time. Restoration has never been more important than it is today.

Information Overload

Technology propels us so fast that we're now expected to communicate almost instantaneously. Jeff Davis is a prolific author who speaks about the information base, which used to double every 15 years. But in the later part of the 20th century, it increased to every five years, and now in the early 21st century, our load doubles nearly every 18 months. What happens to our civilization when so much data is constantly flooding our brains? One thing is for sure: We all feel we should be learning more, doing more, and *being* more. Psychological studies on communicating and resolving stress are crucial in a society where high school violence and road rage have become daily occurrences.

The good news is that cutting edge medicine and nutrition have increased our life expectancy, and alternative medicine now offers new options. But living longer means there's more to learn, so you can make informed decisions. Financial planning and stock market strategies are now necessary for almost everyone, to augment Social Security and savings. And the list goes on and on.

Throughout these chapters I have included quizzes and exercises to prompt self-discovery. Take time to work on them from a reflective place and write the answers in a special notebook. Date the entries so when you look through this material in years to come you will gain perspective. Even if you've done similar work before, ask yourself, "Is more of me ready to be revealed?"

QUIZ: Stress Response Test

The following quiz will help you identify your stress symptoms. When it comes to aging, are you on the fast track to a big slowdown? Answer Yes or No to the following questions:

1. I get headaches easily.

   Yes _____   No _____

2. I have digestive problems.

   Yes _____   No _____

3. I frequently get colds and flu.

   Yes _____   No _____

4. I often have interrupted sleep or insomnia.

   Yes _____   No _____

5. I always feel rushed.

   Yes _____   No _____

6. I drive too fast.

   Yes _____   No _____

7. I drink caffeine throughout the day.

   Yes _____   No _____

8. I eat high fat or sugary foods to boost my energy.

   Yes _____   No _____

9. I'm smoking more or I've recently started smoking again.

Yes _____ No _____

10. I drink more alcohol than I used to.

Yes _____ No _____

11. I often lose my temper.

Yes _____ No _____

12. I can't stop thinking about my problems or "shut off" my busy brain.

Yes _____ No _____

13. I'm carrying a lot of tension in my neck, back, or shoulders.

Yes _____ No _____

14. I don't have the optimism I once had.

Yes _____ No _____

15. I often feel fatigued.

Yes _____ No _____

16. I'm sometimes clumsy, I keep dropping or bumping into things.

Yes _____ No _____

17. I seem to get into more arguments than I used to.

Yes _____ No _____

Count the number of "yes" responses.

Total Score _____

Score 1–2: I am living wisely and have slowed down the aging process. Living life at this pace is comfortable and rewarding.

Score 3–4: I am in need of some solutions to keep me calm. I'm not yet fast-tracking toward old age, but it's time to slow down a bit and see if I can become more effective. I need more quality than quantity in my life.

Score 5–6: My reserves are running low, and solutions to stress need to become a priority. I'm already on the aging fast track, but can easily get back in balance by making some lifestyle changes.

Score 7–8: My reserves are almost empty. I need to implement several lifestyle changes and need to do it *now*. Continuing as I am will keep me on this fast-track-to-aging lifestyle.

Score 9–10: I'm running on empty. I need to take time off to rest, to restore my reserves, and to reevaluate life priorities, so I can implement much-needed change.

Score 11–13: I've been functioning on empty for a while, maybe years. I probably need professional help to restore my health. Acupuncture, massage, and chiropractic therapy are needed for renewal. Taking time off is not a luxury—it's imperative!

In the last couple of years the scores of my audiences have gone up dramatically. The test hasn't changed, but the increased scores clearly indicate how starved we are as a society for a little time off—and time out.

Left- and Right-Brain Functions During Stress

When we are in the midst of chaos, our right brain functioning shuts off and we rely solely on our left brain. Let's look at the qualities of left-brain and right-brain activity:

Left Brain	Right Brain
Language	Shapes
Linear	Holistic
Logical	Intuitive
Digital	Spatial
Abstract	Analogical
Concrete	Symbolic
Reason	Imagination
Analytical	Gestalt
Music–Beat	Music–Melody
Sequential	Sporadic
Time-Bound	Timeless

Some people will be more attracted to right-brain versus left-brain characteristics, but we need both. What happens during stress and overload is that the attributes of the right brain become inaccessible, which means we lose our intuitiveness and imagination. The way to bridge back over to our holistic right brain is to find the calm in the midst of the storm.

Chaos and fear are closely linked. When we shift into a panic state, we fuel the flames of chaos. I love the analogy of "fear storms," because that is what they are. Eventually they blow over just like a storm, if we don't encourage them to stay.

When our abstract, analytical mind grabs hold of a fearful situation, we can be overwhelmed by problems in all areas. Real or imagined, these thoughts activate all our stress hormones. Think back on a situation where you were waiting for a loved one to arrive, and when he or she failed to show up, you began thinking the worst. Suddenly your whole being became upset, restless, and fitful and the tension lasted until your fears were proved unfounded. Sound familiar? When these fear storms take over, we are completely out of the moment.

Choose Your Values Carefully

During a Hawaiian vacation we were in escrow to purchase a new home. I awoke one morning with gut-twisting anxiety over our realtors' attempting to make additional money at our expense by steering us toward their termite contractor and mortgage people, both of whom charged a higher rate—and kicked back a finder's fee.

That year I had learned about the proud Hawaiian people who believed in advancing themselves without costing or harming others. These people lived from such simple principles and their faces showed it. They had the radiant glow of truth and goodness. The infamous quote paraphrased here, "A youthful beauty is a freak accident of nature, but a gracefully aged beauty is a work of art," says it well. The way we live our life shows on our face.

I realized then how much I valued people who conduct their lives in accordance with this principle. I also realized why our realtors—whom I had known casually for years—looked so worn down and out of sorts.

Our aging process speeds up during stressful, sleepless, and frustrated times in our lives. When the *fear storms* or *chaos tornadoes* hit hard, damage control is called for after they finally move on. We need to counter the aging process that kicks into gear when we inadvertently advance ourselves at the cost of another or let the chaos of others rule our lives.

CHAPTER FOUR

Defining Moments

"Life shrinks or expands in proportion to one's courage."

—ANAÏS NIN

We all have life-changing moments that are etched in our memories forever. A marriage proposal, the death of a loved one, or news of a national tragedy become markers in our lives. But there are other events too, that are less definitive yet have impact. A defining moment for one person can be a mere blip on the screen for someone else. One example of this is the well-known "he said, she said" phenomenon, where lovers or spouses may have completely different recollections of the same incident. We see this also when siblings reminisce about a shared childhood. The stories they tell of past occurrences may differ considerably. One sister may remember that Dad was always there for her while another insists he was never around. Or a husband and wife might vacation with another couple, and later the wife may discuss her impression

31

of their friends' marital problems, while her husband may not see any rift at all.

When we compile our responses to a new situation, it is our defining moments that provide a reference point. There are as many viewpoints as there are people. Is it any wonder that communication is often a challenge? What makes defining moments unique is that our vivid impression of them often shapes the direction of our lives. These conclusions become the basis for future responses, and this is where calm and chaos define us.

The Longest Day

One of my defining moments occurred some years ago when I joined my parents in Puerto Vallarta for some much needed R and R. I thought this would be a perfect escape from the pressures of my sales job. Our hotel was right on the ocean and the ambience immediately mellowed me into a blissful state. Unhappy as I was in my career, I figured, "Work is a drag, but as long as I can break away for good times like this I can make it through."

We toured the area and lunched in the quaint village before heading back for an afternoon swim. It was a dazzling Margaritaville sort of day, with smiling, suntanned people frolicking to the sounds of mariachis. I became more relaxed with every breath. With the sparkling surf beckoning to us, Dad and I decided to go for a swim. As soon as we dove into the water, a set of big breakers began to roll in. Having spent many summers by the Great Lakes, bodysurfing was a favorite family pastime. Dad and I joyfully took on the waves, laughing and splashing until a huge one knocked me upside down. When I finally got myself together and raised my head out of the surf, I turned around and noticed that my dad was no longer there.

As I scanned the beach my eyes suddenly caught sight of something floating in the water about 50 yards away. *It couldn't be.* It was too shocking to comprehend. One minute I'd been in a movie-like dreamscape, the whole world warm and wonderful. *That object couldn't be my father. Not him. Not floating facedown.* The adrenaline coursed through my shocked body as I half ran, half stumbled to his side. Refusing to draw a breath of my own, I turned him over. He wasn't breathing. I felt trapped in a slow-motion nightmare, screaming for help as I pulled his six-foot body toward the shore. I kept calling out, yelling out to God and whoever else could hear me for help and divine action. Out of nowhere, a circle of people appeared and heroic efforts were made to bring my father back to life. While someone was performing CPR, I ran toward the hotel, screaming for an ambulance, praying for a miracle.

The breath was back in his body . . . but that's about it.

One of the doctors on the beach had tested the reflexes in my father's legs, and as he suspected, a broken neck was the probable cause of his drowning. The waves sent him crashing headfirst into the sand, snapping the C-4 and C-5 vertebrae in his neck, rendering him paralyzed and utterly helpless. He held on to life five weeks in that condition before he passed away.

Defining moments are what change the course of our lives. In one random instant, the best day of my life suddenly erupted into an explosion of pain and irreversible loss. This experience taught me that no one can be sure of anything beyond the next breath. We have no guarantee that our health will hold up, that our loved ones will escape harm, or that our world itself will remain intact. Knowing how fragile we are and at the same time how strong, I found the courage to ultimately change my life. The final gift my father gave me as I pulled him out of the water that dreadful day was the igniting of my own power, a spiritual bequest passed from father to child.

I had always admired him so. In our codependent relationship, I had given my power away to him in childhood. My overly protective, knows-everything dad could do no wrong. Before he left this earth, he gave this power back to me. I believe that when an entity dies, it leaves a special essence behind. Anyone who has been privileged to witness a death can attest to learning and gaining from the experience. You cannot witness either the beginning of life or its end and not feel a stirring in your soul.

A New Path

We never know exactly where we stand in this journey of life, but defining moments can help clarify our vision. I had known that the trials in my life were helping me evolve into something more than a food broker. I was miserable in my work because I had a burning desire to help people improve their lives and I could wait no longer. Within a year of my father's passing I married for the first time, a miracle in itself. I had passed through my twenties and was heading into my late thirties before I was destined to march down the aisle. What I had learned in the defining moment of my father's death was that in order to change my life I had to *start now*. So when my beloved proposed, I made the commitment to marry without hesitation.

Within months of my marriage, I relinquished the security of my food service position and started my own company. I began teaching others that life satisfaction is a priority, and whatever transformation we must make for this to occur is essential. Just find the *creative life solution*, I told my clients, and go with it.

Some defining moments are less dramatic than others, but every one of these realizations is significant. When we learn that a friend has betrayed us, that a relationship must end, or discover untapped talents within ourselves, our lives are never again quite the same. Defining moments alter our perceptions, attitudes, and beliefs; defining moments shape our lives.

In our efforts to manage chaos and stress, defining moments become our repertoire of resources. We say to ourselves, *If I got through that I can handle anything*.

After a high school shooting where several students were killed or injured, a memorial for the victims was televised locally. As I watched the service, I was struck by the calm demeanor of the high school principal. She was clearly holding back grief and anger; but as she spoke, her message of hope and goodness came through. She emphasized the strength of the community, people from all walks pulling together to face this tragedy. Her demeanor was impressive; you could feel her inner peace in the throes of chaos and tragedy.

EXERCISE: Defining Moments—Crisis You Handled Calmly

How many of you have been through a major crisis in your life when—in the midst of it all—you were able to feel a sense of calm and control? Think about the situation, describe it in detail, and consider your sources of strength. Record the answers in your journal.

Describe the situation:

Why do you think you reacted this way?

What lessons did you learn about yourself?

What success was gained as a result?

EXERCISE: Defining Moments—Crisis That Created Chaos

Have you been through a major ordeal where you were feeling chaotic, restless, and out of control? Describe that situation and to what you attribute your lack of power. As Miles Davis said, "Do not fear mistakes—there are none." Journal on these situations as well.

Describe the situation:

Why do you think you reacted this way?

What lessons did you learn about yourself?

What success was gained as a result?

Building a Stronger Back

Having experienced dire circumstances from both sides of the fence, I decided to devote my life to learning how we can function at a high level when faced with hardships and uncertainty. I also wanted to devise a plan to work this fight-or-flight stress muscle when it is not in use. Even in times of relative calm, we can still strengthen this "crisis muscle" so that it will bolster us in the face of our next challenge. I once heard a quote that I think applies here: "Rather than pray for a lighter load to carry—ask for a stronger back."

Changing the way we respond to stress requires us to review our priorities and life values. This calls for some serious introspection because as defining moments shape our lives, we shift our perspective.

In my early twenties I remember thinking that I wasn't quite sure who I was. I had my father's work ethic and my mother's social skills, but never my own identity. I dressed well like Grandma O and was a first-rate cook like Grandma S. I was articulate like Dad, had a sense of humor like Aunt Elsie, strong opinions like Aunt Marge, and had my mom's ability to inspire confidences. I don't know if this patchwork personality came from other people saying that I reminded them of so and so, or if I just spent too much time focused on appearances and comparisons. I never delved inside to see if there was an original one-of-a-kind *me* in there.

The best decision I ever made was to take the time to do this. I was in my late twenties then and without romantic distractions, I had the time and energy to try to understand myself. During my early years of self-discovery, I met with a minister who had a busy teaching and

counseling schedule. A session with Judith was like bar-
ing your soul before God. At that time I thought I wanted
to become a minister myself and her community church
seemed ideal, but Judith was thinking of closing up shop
in San Diego and moving to Taos. During our work together she suggested I go on a weekend retreat and spend
my time enjoying nature, listening to music, writing, and
reflecting.

Of all Southern California's glorious places, I chose a
mountain resort area near Palm Springs, called Idyllwild.
I brought all I needed for the weekend—food, books, and
music—and I checked into a cozy little cabin. But instead
of finding serenity, I became so anxious after the first night
alone that I spent most of the next two days in town shopping and making small talk with clerks. On Sunday
afternoon as I prepared to leave, I realized I hadn't done
much but shop and cavort around town, pretty much unable to spend time alone. The one book I read that
weekend was *You Can Heal Your Life* by Louise Hay. It was
riveting. It was a calling-card experience that gave me a
hopeful glimpse into my future. As I read Ms. Hay's work
and walked in the woods, I knew this was the kind of future I envisioned for myself.

As uplifted as I felt by this book and the beauty of
Idyllwild, I didn't consider the weekend a success because
I hadn't completed my assignment. My reason for going
in the first place was to get acquainted with the essence of
my spirit, but I'd hardly spent any time on my own.

Why did I feel so uncomfortable being by myself? What
was I resisting? I knew I had to find out more.

So I went back to Idyllwild. More than once. Each
time I stayed at the same place, and each time I ended up

spending more time solo and pursuing my quest, via journaling, reading, hiking, and sometimes just staring into the fire. My search was eventually rewarded by new insights and answers. Did I dare tell anyone how much I enjoyed just doing nothing? Just being. Just breathing. Just talking to myself, to God, and sometimes crying. My best days of self-discovery were those when I had no plans, just going with the flow, where one thing led to the next. I would meet with serendipity when I lived this way and followed my inner source. This really is who I am at my best. Visiting this mountain resort changed my life and I continue to go on these spiritual retreats even now.

I know it has taken me many years of search and research, and this is just a beginning. Anytime I discover a new facet of myself I feel like I've hit the lottery. I'm not talking about surface roles of parent, employee, business owner, volunteer, or student. Those are superficial, just roles. I'm talking about the qualities that make a good parent; a sense of responsibility, maturity, and patience, among others. And what makes a good entrepreneur? Vision, expertise, and knowledge. These are defining statements about our character, not just job titles.

For example, I'm now a professional speaker, but as a speaker I might be outgoing, intelligent, as well as entertaining, helpful, hardworking, understanding, and honest. Or I may be a speaker who is entertaining, outgoing, and intelligent, but also manipulative, egotistical, and deceitful. So the job title does not tell us much about the individual. It is the qualities of character that define who we are.

The Better I Know Myself, The Better I Show Myself

When I know who I am, tranquility and confidence come naturally. When I know who I am, crises, chaos, and challenging situations can be resolved more easily. When I maintain my faith in trying times, people seem to show up out of nowhere to offer assistance.

Your words are your entry point into the reality of your life. Your thoughts preface your words, but listen to what you say in times of crisis and uncertainty. Do you give the world a picture of confidence? Or do your words convey a negative outlook and lack of trust? A victim mentality tends to create more chaos. When you hear yourself going in this direction, tighten your reins and pull back. Inner victims create lives of chaos; inner warriors run lives of calm. Which course do you want to take?

As children trying to please Mom or Dad, we learn early on to satisfy others. However, a life of doing what's expected or what others dictate rarely serves our best interest. If we thrive on social situations, then perhaps that hotshot computer job isn't the best choice, no matter how proud and comfortable it makes our loved ones. Sales, customer service, or teaching might be a better fit for extroverts. We need to know what makes us happy. How can we please ourselves if we don't know what we truly want or like?

With the recent shift toward finding spiritual meaning in our lives, we hear a lot about the importance of self-understanding. "To thine own self be true." A nun recently published a book called *10 Fun Things to Do Before You Die*. Her list of must-dos included gaining insight and finding one's best self. Some may choose to do this by living alone for a time, for solitude has much to teach us. If you share a household, find a place where you can go off by yourself and escape from your daily routine. This is a way we "find" ourselves.

QUIZ: What Matters Most?

Here is a warm-up exercise with a point. Take the following quiz and see how you score.

Name five of the wealthiest people in the world.

Name five Heisman Trophy winners.

Name five winners of the Miss America or Miss Universe title.

Name five people who have won the Nobel or Pulitzer Prize.

How about five or 10 Academy Awards winners?

Other than the New York Yankees, name five World Series–winning teams.

How did you do? For the categories that were easy for you, these are your passions. With the exception of you trivia hounds, most of us don't remember many of yesterday's headliners. It's surprising how quickly we forget. What I've asked about aren't obscure achievements.

These awards represent the best and brightest in their respective fields. But when the applause is over, awards tarnish, achievements are forgotten, and trophies are buried with their owners.

QUIZ: People That Matter Most

Name three people you enjoy spending time with.

Name five people who have taught you something worthwhile.

Name five friends who have helped you during a difficult time.

List three of your favorite teachers.

Name three heroes whose stories have inspired you.

Was this quiz easier to take? Sure it was. The reason is that the people who make the greatest difference are not the ones with credentials, but those with compassion and concern. People whose lives are materially focused may not understand the payoff in such work. It involves being reflective, vulnerable, and sometimes enduring emotional storms.

EXERCISE: Lessons from Memory

You are one of a kind. There is not another like you in this universe. You are also the only one who will ever fully realize who you are, what your capabilities and weaknesses are, and only you will truly know the levels of every emotion you experience. For me, the key to life is in knowing myself, my talents and my limitations, so I can better work and contribute to the world. And, oh the stress we save ourselves when we gain self-knowledge!

List your three to five most significant memories from ages 1 to 10.

What lesson(s) did you learn from this first decade?

List your most significant memories from age 11 to 20.

What lesson(s) did you learn from this decade?

List your most significant memories from age 21 to 30.

What lesson(s) did you learn from this decade?

List your most significant memories from age 31 to 40.

What lessons did you learn from this decade?

List your most significant memories from age 41 to 50.

What lessons did you learn from this decade?

List your most significant memories from age 51 to 60.

What lessons did you learn from this decade?

List your most significant memories from age 61 to 70.

What lessons did you learn from this decade?

List your most significant memories from age 71 to 80.

What lessons did you learn from this decade?

(Complete for each decade to your current age. P.S. Congratulations on living this long!)

EXERCISE: A Check-up from the Neck Up

Compare the two columns below and circle which of the two choices best describes you. There are no "right" or "wrong" answers.

Thoughtful	Impulsive
Serious	Humorous
Physical	Intellectual
Artistic	Scientific

Spiritual	Material
Self-oriented	Other-oriented
Care-giving	Love pampering
Initiator	Observant
Personable	Standoffish
Arrogant	Modest
Confident	Insecure
Big picture–oriented	Detail-oriented
Have firm boundaries	Tendency to be a doormat
Nature lover	City slicker
Enthusiastic	Apathetic
Happy	Depressed
Mischievous	Pious
Cautious	Risk-taker
Boring	Interesting
Shy	Outgoing
Dreamer	Doer
Resourceful	Wasteful
Engaging	Alienating
Restless	Peaceful
Kind	Mean-spirited
Type "A" Personality	Laid-back
Authentic	Phony
Leader	Follower
Goal-oriented	Fatalistic
Optimist	Pessimist
Gregarious	Solitary
Cup is half full	Cup is half empty
Well-coordinated	Klutzy
Aggressive	Passive
No-nonsense type	Whimsical

Why We Thrive—Why We Hide

After doing this exercise, we begin to see a pattern; we tend to be methodical or spontaneous, introverted or extroverted, practical or visionary, artistic or numeric. With this in mind we can begin to see why, in certain situations or with certain people, we often thrive—or we hide. The better we know ourselves the more we can choose situations and relationships that are in our best interest. For some, this may be just common sense, although innate wisdom is not common at all. If we have fallen into a pattern of destructive situations and relationships, we need to free ourselves from our old blueprint.

For example, if a teacher or parent implies that you aren't any good at math, science, or whatever, it often becomes a self-fulfilling prophecy. I'm not suggesting that we all have the talents of Picasso or Einstein, but I am saying we can probably complete a class or project in these areas where we were deemed unworthy, and in doing so get a tremendous rush of self-confidence and respect.

How do we release old patterns? Like all worthy ventures, it takes some doing. We must have the willingness to widen our self-perceptions, and this can be painful. But if we keep hiding and avoiding challenges, we'll never realize that it's not others who limit us and cause suffering, but our own insights, biases, and ego or lack of ego. Some things in life are beyond our control, but we *can* change ourselves.

Starting now.

CHAPTER FIVE

Keys to Calm

"Self-reverence, self-knowledge, self-control—
these three alone lead to success."
—ALFRED LORD TENNYSON

I was wrestling with a trauma I had carried with me since childhood. Several years back I'd been doing some work in this area when John Bradshaw made a coup in the recovery field with his bestseller, *Healing the Shame That Binds You.* I wanted to understand my role in my family and so I was doing some serious investigating. I learned in the process that blaming your parents or others is a pointless way to live. No one is perfect and we all have something to learn from our family members, because they are ultimately our most insightful teachers.

I always resonated with the idea that there are two categories of people: friends and teachers. Your friends love and support you through good times and bad. Your teachers, on the other hand, point out your areas of weakness through a lack of support, criticism, or even rejection. The point is, we have no enemies as such. When we think of those who betray, deceive, and manipulate us as *teachers*, this is a wonderful philosophical way to overcome resentment and anger. If I think I'm having a bad day because more than three "teachers" have appeared to point out my limitations, chances are the problem has to do with my own perceptions, and I know I shouldn't cast blame.

I once had a rejection issue that illustrates this point. When I was growing up, my family bonded through sports, and golf was the big favorite. I began swinging a club at the tender age of six, and although I was no Tiger Woods, I did inherit my father's natural swing. This proficiency prompted my family to keep me in the game even though I made it clear that golf wasn't my idea of a good time.

There were other sports too, such as skiing and tennis, where I was dragged along, grumbling all the way because I felt my family was rejecting the true me. They didn't know how—or care enough—to accommodate my more reflective artistic interests. At one point as a teenager, my mother did try to encourage me to try acting, something for which I had a natural flair. But by that time I was deeply caught up in my feelings of rejection and I turned down the opportunity. Even after I left home, I was so conditioned to this rejection response that I unwittingly perpetuated the pattern. It was only after years of soul-searching that I understood how profoundly these patterns affect our lives.

This is why I counsel people on managing stress. Through my own life and investigations, I have come to realize that most stress patterns are self-inflicted. If we can unhook these old patterns of rejection and denial, we can attain a new sense of calm and freedom. In fact, various religions and social groups provide ways to accomplish this process: Catholics go to confession, Jews perform annual rituals of assessment and review, and 12-step program members take a personal inventory.

Self-investigation takes a lot of hard work. And for most of us that means "time out." If you are always in a time crunch, you may miss this aspect of life, which in my humble opinion, is what makes it all meaningful.

A Friend and Mentor

I was 28 years old when I met him. Ken was a 70-year-old man who had quit drinking a decade earlier. I loved to be around him, for he exuded a kind of calm that I could feel just walking into his home. He loved God. One of his favorite books was *Practicing the Presence* by Joel Goldsmith. I felt the Presence when I was with Ken. But sadly, our time together would be all too brief.

Ken held a study group in his home on Monday nights. Several of us read books together, followed by spirited discussions. We read the works of Joel Goldsmith, Og Mandino, Vernon Howard, and the wonderful Ernest Holmes. During this time I was actually studying to be a practitioner of Ernest Holmes' teachings, but didn't even know it.

Ken's death was a significant defining moment for me. I lived next door to him the last nine months of his life. At the close of the Memorial Day weekend, our class ended as usual, with hugs all around, and we left Ken alone, unaware of any problems. The next morning his window shades failed to go up. At lunchtime I noticed this and thought perhaps he'd slept in. But by mid-afternoon I knew something was wrong.

I ran next door and let myself into Ken's house with the emergency key. When I called his name and he didn't respond, I feared the worst. But when I walked into the bedroom and found his body, the scene was so peaceful that I thought, *This is how a spiritual passing looks. This is the way I want to live—and die.* Even in death, Ken taught me how to surrender to that higher force that organizes the universe and our world.

How to Use Journaling to Reduce Stress

Some of you might laugh when I suggest that you write about the things that are stressing you. The idea that there is any time to write about the problems of an over-scheduled life seems absurd. I used to always dial up my friends to discuss my latest upset rather than taking the time to sit down and write about it. Then one day I heard the "magic formula," and I learned why writing this "stuff" out is such good therapy.

I was at a meeting in Hawaii, and a speaker explained that when we talk about our problems we engage about 100,000 nerve cells in the process. But when we put our thoughts on paper, we activate something like 2,000,000 cells! The combination of visual and manual processes engages the brain 20 times more than mere lip service.

EXERCISE: External and Internal Stressors

One of my longtime clients is a computer engineer who always schedules time to attend Day of Healing seminars. She shared her methodical and effective system of taking inventory of her various stressors. Drawing a line down the middle of a page in her journal, she listed external and internal pressures in separate columns. It looked something like this:

External Stressor	Internal Stressor
Being a Single Parent	Unresolved Relationship Issues
Job Change	Financial Worries
Uncomfortable Living Conditions	Feelings of Insecurity
Legal Entanglements	Desire to Leave Past Behind
Unfriendly Neighbors	Yearning for a Gentler Way of Life

This simple exercise helps put our problems into focus. Most of the things in the left column are beyond our control. The items on the right, however, describe the way we *feel* about the pressures in our lives, and that is something we *can* change. Just writing down and acknowledging what our stressors are is a positive action. If you can share your concerns with a trusted friend it makes your load still less of a burden.

Itemize your external and internal stressors and see if this formula works for you. Remember it's the items on the right you want to reframe. (see page 104 for more information)

Unloading Our Baggage

Sometimes we need to revisit the past to relieve ourselves of stress we are carrying around from too many yesterdays. When we are coping with any kind of loss, we often muscle our way through until the pain diminishes or the situation and feelings begin to shift. But by coping this way we don't fully experience our emotional upheavals, and they never fully leave us. We continue to reference *that marriage, that year,* or *that job* with distress because we haven't healed our perspective of the situation.

If you keep accumulating these unresolved issues, you end up carrying an elephant-sized load. You don't know why you've lost your zest for life. You might remember feeling freer when you were younger and begin to lament your lost youth. But guess what? You haven't lost your youth; you've just lost touch with the lighthearted joys of an earlier time.

Understanding our emotional patterns can help us in navigating a calmer life. Let's say you're someone who always has to be number one. You are uncomfortable at meetings or social events where someone else is in the limelight. A great way to gain a new perspective is to attend an event as an observer or allow someone else to control the evening. If you feel you're wasting your time when you are *not* the guest of honor, ask yourself why you always need the spotlight. What part of you has this driving need for attention? Can you find some value in situations without crowds, applause, and attention? Can you still love yourself when you're not number one?

When we lighten up and release these painful accumulations, we are more open to what life has to offer. Opportunities come our way when we are receptive and, trust me, colleagues, friends, and loved ones can sense when we are walled off by old baggage. When we learn to release this inner turmoil, we can then walk into a business meeting, a party, or a public arena and share our lightness with the world. We are the calm in the midst of chaos. People want to know us, they want to hire us, and they want to love us.

When we start to retrace these painful accumulations called "energy cysts" (i.e., blocks), and allow them to leave us mentally, emotionally, and spiritually, that is the moment we become lighter and more youthful. I call this process *healing*, and this is exactly the process that shifted my own life from one of upheaval to one of joy.

The Music of Healing

I once knew a terrific guy, a businessman with a serious weight problem. He tipped the scale at nearly 300 pounds and was astounded when I told him that his cravings for greasy hamburgers and donuts could be eased if he dealt with his emotional and spiritual baggage. Some time after that I ran into him again. He was talking about how he had found the *Kabala*, and how excited he was spending full days in study. He didn't have to say more. I knew this was the beginning of the end of his addiction to rich foods, and the start of a healthier and happier life.

I also worked with a financial planner who had multiple sclerosis as well as other health problems. She kept going to doctors who treated her symptoms surgically. She was cut up like a patchwork quilt from operations on her stomach, pancreas, and gallbladder. The procedures were performed because her organs were shutting down. During our session I saw that her heart was clearly blocked. I dialogued with her and finally said, "When did you put a shield around your heart?"

Startled, she replied, "My mother died when I was 10 and as we buried her, I told myself I never wanted to love anyone again. I felt if I loved someone they would leave me."

"Your internal organs are shutting down because you've cut yourself off from love," I told her. "We need love to survive. Love fuels every cell and system in our bodies." Her body was deteriorating and she was "dying" from this lack of love and trust.

Through her tears she murmured, "I just can't let someone in and let myself be loved."

I smiled. "It's too late, I've been loving you since the moment you came in here today."

Suddenly her body began to respond. As this block was lifted from her heart, her organs started to reactivate. It sounded like a symphony. The stomach played, then the spleen, then the pancreas, liver, and intestines. It was the most amazing orchestra of healing as all these organs were set in motion and began to play. It was the music of healing I heard that day.

It is common for those who have unhealed grief to try to shield their heart. The problem is that many of us leave the shield in place for the rest of our lives and never fully open our hearts to love. Heart shields are like armor and can be the origin of heart disease, if a person keeps that love and hurt bottled inside.

As I was doing my own inner explorations, I found a common theme to the chaos I was experiencing and realized that I had a tendency to overreact. It didn't matter who or what was going on around me, I always spun things into a crisis. I initially attributed this drama-queen pattern to my innate sensitivity. But after exhausting all my rationalizations about my gifts of awareness, I concluded that I obviously was getting some kind of payoff from making glaciers out of ice cubes. Focused and determined, I decided to tackle my own "inner landscape" and surrender to life's lessons.

If I took in each "trauma"—each experience that upset me—with awe and wonder, I might learn something. Now I replace anger with wonder and ask, "I wonder why this is happening to me?" I can even take my right index finger and point it to my heart as I ask, "I wonder why?" Wondering is a peaceful approach and significant key to calm. It's also a way to be receptive and open to answers. If I did it, you can too.

CHAPTER SIX

Life's Priorities: First Things First

"Let your advance worrying become advance thinking and planning."

—WINSTON CHURCHILL

How you spend your time is how you live your life. If you think time management is passé, you are in denial. The only true equality we have on this planet is our allotment of time. We all have the same 1,440 minutes each day, and nobody gets one nanosecond more, no matter who you know. And how we spend our 24/7s is what defines us.

In my late thirties I learned about the importance of living life according to my own priorities. After my first burnout my emphasis shifted to health and helping others, rather than money, power, and prestige (MPP). I still wanted success and recognition, but my life was now about doing some good in the world rather than taking a cut-throat approach to my competition.

When values shift, priorities change. The second time I burned out because I'd changed my whole inner structure, but was still humdrumming along in the same unsatisfying career. And that's when my story takes an almost comical turn. As I mentioned, food had always been one of my coping mechanisms, so of course I was a walking-talking poster child for my products. If I couldn't relate effectively, if my mood was kicking me to the curb, I'd just feed my face and feel better.

But when I went from the catering business into food sales, I decided I'd rather have an attractive, healthy body than a love/hate relationship with food. For the first time in my life, food was no longer my first priority. And for me a big part of this equation was giving up sugar. So here I was with my new commitment, and meanwhile back at the ranch, I was supposed to be doing what they call "food cuttings." A food cutting is where you sample the new items you're going to be selling, so you can rave about each product's benefit, ingredients, and so forth. Basically you sit around and stuff your face with French fries, desserts, and pizzas and talk food all day—and get paid for it. *Nobody said life is fair!* But now, with my new outlook, my mantra became "No, thank you."

The Impressive Mr. Hobbs

When priorities shift due to health problems or other wake-up calls, we sometimes do a turnaround when we realize that our life has gone off track. For example, if you're in a marriage for reasons other than love and suddenly discover that love is what you really want, then you need to make a change. Change forces us to revisit the principles we uphold and the thoughts we entertain.

The work of Charles Hobbs, a time-management guru in the '80s, focuses on identifying life values and priorities. His work with implementing time-management tactics was adopted by Day-Timer® who partnered with Hobbs in teaching his programs to corporate clients.

Every one of us can benefit from learning these valuable techniques. According to Mr. Hobbs' philosophy, the first step in managing one's time is to identify life values and priorities, which he calls *unifying principles*. Once you affirm them, you then schedule your time with respect to those values and goals. In his book *Time Power*, Mr. Hobbs states, "If you know what you want to achieve and you schedule your time to accommodate your goal, you will accomplish it."

I was impressed with Mr. Hobbs' approach to time, and recognized that his philosophy was critical to managing stress and staying focused in times of chaos. I eventually became a certified trainer for Day-Timer® and started to incorporate these programs as part of my work. When presenting seminars to executives, managers, and frontline personnel, I always allow ample time for participants to identify their unifying principles and priorities. If people really follow this model of scheduling their time, they can be assured that success will follow. I know from personal experience this is essential to job satisfaction and life fulfillment.

Create Your Own "One Page"

My seminar participants always enjoy sharing their own lists of unifying principles. Most of us enjoy telling others what we stand for, if given the chance. One executive used a tool he called his "One Page." He wrote all his life values on a single sheet of paper, and when he was interviewing managers or making important decisions, he would refer to it before taking action. He showed his managers his One Page so they would know where he stood, and suggested they create their own.

If you decide to follow his lead, don't just *think* about your values and priorities—tattoo them on your arm, or at least jot them down in ink. When it comes to our dreams, goals, and priorities, we need to be definitive. Writing them down is a contract we make with ourselves. We then create a permanent record to refer to when we start to waffle, and that in itself is an important step toward attaining our goals.

For more life satisfaction, write your Unifying Principles. They are the core values you use as a guide to living. Examples are: Family, Personal Integrity, Healthy Lifestyle, Spiritual Growth, Education, Honesty, Financial Success, Respect in Community, etc.

Ready...Set...Write down what *you* stand for, and don't forget to write the date.

EXERCISE: My Unifying Principles

_____

_____

_____

_____

_____

_____

_____

_____

_____

_____

_____

_____

_____

_____

_____

_____

_____

_____

CHAPTER SEVEN

Why Do We Fight Eating Right?

*"To keep the body in good health is a duty...
otherwise we shall not be able to keep our
mind strong and clear."*

—BUDDHA

Because so many of the symptoms of stress are physical, the solutions need to be physical too. How we fuel our bodies is always important, but in times of high stress it is critical. And yet it's when we're under pressure that we're most likely to resort to fast foods and sweets, when what we really need is a diet that's natural and nutritious: fruits, vegetables, meats, fish, grains, legumes, and nuts.

The more a food is processed, the more it's depleted of nutrition. We need the fully fortified natural foods to deliver vitamins and minerals in an easily assimilated form. Ideally, 75 percent of our diet should come from natural foods because our bodies are designed to digest them in their fundamental form. Refined or highly processed foods often dump sugar into the bloodstream too quickly, and the result can be fluctuating insulin levels that further stress our bodies and affect our mood and energy.

Going Natural

If you're currently living on a diet of fast food and pizza, you can start with eating 30-50 percent natural foods. Soon you'll begin to feel increased energy and well-being. Whatever enables you to function on a high level and live comfortably should be your goal. In time you may wish to increase your natural food intake to an ideal of 50 to 80 percent.

During my years in sales, I sold frozen and convenience foods in the wholesale food business. I was in a position to see firsthand how many hidden ingredients are used to enhance the flavor and shelf life of processed foods. For example, plain frozen chicken breasts are usually injected with a salt solution to add flavor. If the chicken is seasoned, it likely contains more than one form of sugar and salt, in addition to the injected ingredients. Because sugar and salt appeal to our taste buds, you'll find them in almost every prepared product on the shelf. But while excess is unhealthy, the natural sugars in fruits and grains are a source of energy, and the salts that occur naturally in vegetables, such as high-sodium celery, are essential for keeping our bodies' electrolytes in balance.

One of the perks of my food broker job was a pantry full of free samples. I already mentioned my struggle with 40 pounds of killer chocolates. But it didn't stop there. Everything I sold was available to me, and this meant substantially lowering my grocery bills. We represented a nationally recognized brand of frozen entrees, and when I first got the job I thought I'd hit the jackpot! My refrigerator was soon stocked with frozen lasagnas, macaroni and cheese, manicotti, chicken tenders, and other goodies.

After eating these foods regularly for about three months, I seemed to be getting more colds and flu. After six months I noticed that my normal enthusiasm and energy were on a downswing. The affects of these nutritionally depleted foods were taking a toll. When I started cooking for myself and eating natural foods, my energy, mood, and performance all improved!

Getting the White Out

All the nutritionists I've interviewed believe a healthy diet is one that is relatively free of white sugar and white flour. Some say eliminate all "whites," and that includes dairy foods as well. Why are the experts so down on these popular foods? One reason is that sugar robs the body of its natural calcium. Its high calorie content provides no nutrition, and it stimulates the pancreas so that insulin is dumped into the bloodstream, causing blood sugar levels to fluctuate out of balance.

While dairy products are touted as a good source of calcium, their lactic acid content can leach calcium from the bone, canceling out the benefit. In spite of the ubiquitous "Every body needs milk" ads, milk is considered by many to be unnecessary after the first year of life. Cows have three stomachs and even they can't digest it. And most dairy products contain high levels of hormones which may be carcinogenic and could affect our own hormonal balance. If these things concern you, you may want to eat calcium-rich foods such as salmon or broccoli and take a good, readily absorbed supplement. Or, if you insist on having some dairy in your diet, there are a number of organic and/or hormone-free brands on the market. Your local health food store is the place to find these organic dairy products—and don't forget soymilk, almond milk, or rice milk as a great alternative.

Examine the Fine Print

Of all the reading you do on the subject of food, labels may be the most important. Before you toss an item into your shopping cart, take time to check out its fat and sugar content as well as its list of ingredients. The words you can't pronounce are usually the preservatives and chemical additives. We know that stress alone affects hormones, sleep patterns, and energy levels. If we fuel our bodies with lots of highly processed foods, we only intensify the problem.

Coronary heart disease is our nation's leading cause of death. We all know people who, having survived a first heart attack, are told to change their habits, particularly with regard to eating less salt and saturated fats. But you need to beware of labels that boast "no salt added," or "less fat," or "reduced calories." These big-print claims are meant to attract those seeking healthy foods, but all too often such statements, while technically accurate, are misleading.

For example, in a glass of "2% fat" milk (98% fat-free), about a third of the calories are derived from fat. That's a far cry from something that is truly fat-free. And "no salt added" products may still contain high levels of sodium.

Forget the hype on the front of the can or package and read the small print on the back. You may wish to set your own limits, but a good guideline is three-or-less fat grams, and under 200 grams of sodium per serving.

You Don't Have to Go It Alone

A friend of mine in the food business had a heart attack when he was only 50. He dearly loved his wife and 12-year-old daughter, so he was strongly motivated to change his life. His doctor recommended a low fat diet with lots of fruits and vegetables. John was diligent, and within six months he lost about 30 pounds and looked a decade younger. He considered himself a saved man and told everyone how good he felt.

Unfortunately this is not the end of the story. A few years later I ran into John again and saw immediately that he had gone back to his old eating habits—lots of high fat and refined foods. All the weight had returned and that healthy, revitalized glow was just a memory. When we chatted he told me, "I'm disgusted with myself. I hate what I'm doing, but I've got such a sweet tooth." Once John started eating occasional desserts, his new eating plan went right down the tubes.

When someone who's had such a dramatic wake-up call can't manage to stay on a healthy course, there is usually an emotional issue or attachment to food that needs to be addressed. Experts refer to this as an eating disorder and therapy groups, one-on-one counseling, and organizations such as Weight Watchers have proved highly effective for millions with this kind of problem. Twelve-step programs (which operate on an anonymous, donation-only basis) help those with food addictions and compulsive eating by providing spiritual solutions and fellowship with like-minded people. All the support groups I've attended gave me great insights, but what sustained me through the toughest times was the circle of friends I acquired in these programs.

One of these true-blue friends was a woman who started a support meeting for food addicts in San Diego in the early '90s. Years have gone by and we both still abstain from sugar, wheat, and flour. Plus we still check in by phone to talk about how our lives are going and how we're controlling our longings for food. This special rapport has stood the test of time and has done more for me than any one-on-one therapy or support group.

Diet Is a Four-Letter Word

I spent over two decades of my life dieting in one fashion or another, until I finally realized—just as I'd always heard—*diets don't work*. You have to make a lifestyle change, and it must be one you can live with. But for a long time I couldn't quite figure out exactly what this meant. Once I grasped the concept, it became my full-time passion. This enthusiasm helped me become more effective in all aspects of my life.

I don't recommend that everyone abstain from sugar, wheat, and flour in order to better manage stress. However if you find yourself craving foods like cookies, muffins, pizza, and ice cream, and if these indulgences leave you feeling lethargic or depressed, you may want to consider a lifestyle change as disciplined as mine. My tip-off was that once I started eating certain foods like these, I had to finish the whole package, carton, or amount to be satisfied. Of all the goals I have achieved in my life, living in a normal-sized body day after day is my biggest accomplishment.

For most people, getting a good balance of natural foods and keeping the quick-fix processed stuff to a minimum will provide a buffer against stress and protection against illness.

Our society seems to place a greater value on status, power, and wealth than on good health. But people who drive hard and fast to achieve all the above often end up trading their health for the thrill of the chase. Our bodies are like machines, and modern medicine notwithstanding, this is one vehicle we won't be replacing any time soon. So give yourself a minute and consider what kind of fuel you're using to get through this once-in-a-lifetime journey. Are you pampering yourself like a pricey new Lexus or are you allowing yourself to run on empty?

QUIZ: The Fuel Test

Answer the following questions Yes or No.

1. I usually eat three to five serving of fruits and vegetables every day.   Yes _____   No _____

2. I usually refrain from junk or snack foods I'm craving.   Yes _____   No _____

3. I eat a variety of foods each week, and I rarely eat the same meals day after day.   Yes _____   No _____

4. I eat three to five meals per day.   Yes _____   No _____

5. I rarely skip meals.   Yes _____   No _____

6. I'm aware how much protein is recommended for my body size and type, and I usually get the proper amount.

Yes _____   No _____

7. I make time to eat meals during the day so I don't play catch-up and snack at night when I'm at home.

Yes _____   No _____

8. I do *not* rely on soft drinks or coffee to boost my energy.

Yes _____   No _____

The more "yes" answers, the higher your standard of excellence for your life vehicle. To improve your health and energy, start with one question and make the change indicated until you have a "yes" answer.

About 58 million people in the U.S. have hypertension, a major risk factor for heart disease, and nearly one million cancer cases are diagnosed every year. Thirty-four million adults are obese and the numbers of overweight children are increasing. I am certain there is a correlation between the way we manage stress and our relationship with food. Some people gorge themselves when stressed, while others skip meals and live on snacks because they're too hassled to shop and prepare proper meals. Chronic stress makes for difficult digestion because the body's adrenaline keeps the sympathetic nervous system activated, which consumes energy necessary for proper digestion to occur. Eating and relaxation need to go together, at least once or twice a day.

If you don't find cooking easy or pleasurable, find a good local restaurant or market that offers healthy take-outs. The food business, as the saying goes, has come a long way, baby. Today when you order out, your choices go way beyond pizza and Chinese. There are an abundance of options, from healthy fast-food chains to mom-and-pop delis that offer healthful, low-calorie entrees—and some even deliver. So drop the "I'm too busy to cook" routine and get out the Yellow Pages. The important thing is to always make the healthy decision to eat right, especially when stress and time demands are high. It's never been easier.

CHAPTER EIGHT

Don't Rationalize— Exercise!

"Exercise is for Everybody."
—THE AMERICAN MEDICAL ASSOCIATION

One of the great gifts my mother gave me was the love of exercise. Having had rheumatic fever twice in her childhood, she was bedridden for months at a time. Surviving that, she became a fitness-minded adult. Not only was she athletic in her hobbies of skiing, golfing, tennis, and tai chi, she also studied karate for 15 years and became a second degree black belt at 62. She enjoys her morning jog, yoga, swimming, or whatever physical activity she pursues.

Exercise is a living meditation. When you feel sluggish, tired, or depressed, move the body and the mind will follow. Thirty minutes to an hour, three to four times a week is all you need to increase your vitality and gain a sense of accomplishment. Some studies even show that regular exercise can reduce your physical age by as much as 20 years. *If there's a fountain of youth—this is it.* That said, let's explore the various types of exercise, to see which is best tailored to your particular goals.

Certain types of movements are designed to promote renewal and inner peace. In general, Western workouts have traditionally been more about tightening and sculpting muscles, while Eastern forms of exercise focus on toning and relaxation. When you carve out time in your schedule for keeping fit, what is your goal? To tighten up or to relax? Or both?

The Best from the West

Different personality and body types tend to benefit from different strategies. I have a friend who releases all her angst after a strenuous aerobics class. She enjoys dance and high-impact movement, so for her this works fine. Other people prefer weight training, which is the ultimate "tightening" exercise. Jack La Lanne was the weight lifting pioneer of the '50s. He emphasized fitness as a key to successful living and was always pushing the limits with his own body. When he opened his first gym, people gossiped that his ideas were strange. He wanted to help celebrities and top executives, but they scoffed at his ideas of weight lifting and fitness. Instead he took his gospel of fitness to overweight youths and began to make a difference. The word got out; with his inspirational message his became one of the first exercise programs on TV. Who can forget Jack and his chair exercises? I saw him at a fitness convention and he touched my life in one simple hour. He was also an advocate for no-sugar living. He told the audience, "Sugar will make you insane."

Pumping iron came into the limelight again when Oprah "made the connection" with Bob Greene. Lots of people followed suit and hired personal trainers, and the "boom" is still in full swing. Although weight training doesn't promote relaxation, as do Eastern disciplines, it does provide significant benefits.

If you choose to do some heavy lifting, you'll strengthen your bones and build muscle. The latter will speed up your metabolism because muscles burn fat even while you're sleeping. And as an added bonus, strong muscles and bones reduce the risk of injury and accidents. There are social benefits too, when you work out in a gym. Many people enjoy the camaraderie found in health clubs and exercise classes. It's easier when we work out with others or find a partner to keep us committed. The popular American formula seems to be weight training combined with aerobics for cardiovascular health.

Besides aerobics classes, another fun way to work out is Jazzercise: a choreographed aerobics/jazz dance class. The founder, Judi Sheppard Missett, and her international organization have a mission: to bring the joy of jazz dance to the world as a way to keep fit. Knowing most people don't have the necessary discipline of a dancer, Judi simplified jazz dance moves to music and choreographed what has become known as Jazzercise. These classes are plenty of fun, let you express as a dancer, and are challenging.

Wisdom from the East

The recent popularity of Eastern forms of exercise demonstrates that we Western go-getters may need a change of pace. Yoga, Tai Chi, Chi Gong, and Pilates are available at health clubs throughout the country. Many nationwide chains offer Hatha Yoga or a Western-like form of Power Yoga. We in America are notorious for taking time-honored practices and modernizing them to better suit our needs. Hence Power Yoga is sort of a push-yourself, atta-girl form of the ancient discipline.

I happen to prefer the more unadulterated styles of Yoga or Tai Chi. Since these forms of exercise have stood the test of time, sign me up.

Yoga and Tai Chi are the world's oldest forms of mental and physical discipline. The Yogic philosophy is one of compassion and connecting with the inner peace that resides in us all. When you do the Yoga postures you are opening up your body to activate the life force and quiet the mind. Breathing is a key to mental tranquility, and as you do the *asanas* (Yoga postures) slow deep breathing is part of the "dance." *Ashtanga* Yoga is about increasing the heat in the body and burning away toxins. Yoga helps to break the negative cycles of the mind that have become chronic thought patterns we fall in love with, even if they're destructive.

Hatha Yoga is a gentler form of the discipline, popular in this country, involving more stretching and relaxation techniques. All forms of Yoga are designed to bring us into a state of enlightenment, which is why the Yogis have practiced them for centuries. Now, in the information age, we have an abundance of resources to help us reach this enlightened state, but we don't always take advantage of them.

The Chinese have mastered the use of *chi*. Chi is an energy force within us all. The reservoir of chi is located one inch below the naval and one inch deep in the abdomen. Chinese philosophy teaches that the greater the chi (life force) the healthier the person and the greater his chances for longevity. For thousands of years the Chinese have practiced Tai Chi with the intention of cultivating the internal life force. The exercises are performed in a standing position, and involve very slow specific movements with names like *poses like crane* and *grasping bird with tail*. Tai Chi is poetry in motion; just watching a class will relax you. The benefits are exponentially greater for those who participate.

Chi Gong is a similar system of activating the life force, but it isn't quite as poetic as the slow chi dance of Tai Chi. Chi Gong works with meridians of the body. When these energy channels are clear and open, they easily distribute the chi throughout the body. Healthy chi, healthy body. Restricted meridians lead to decreased energy, and lower immune function. Chi Gong can help people with arm and leg problems.

The Best of All Worlds

No one else can decide which exercise program is "right" for you. But just as your body benefits from a varied diet, you'll find advantages in trying different types of workouts. If you've never taken a Yoga class, you can easily find one at your neighborhood gym or recreation center. If you discover you enjoy a beginner's class, you may wish to branch out into something more challenging like Pilates. Or you might want to shake up your routine with a gymnastics class or some team basketball. Jumping on a trampoline, swinging a bat, or riding the waves on a boogie board are all great antidotes to exercise boredom. The most important thing is to keep your body in motion. Whatever you enjoy is what you'll do. Exercise should be a three-letter word, because we don't make excuses when we're having f-u-n.

CHAPTER NINE

Alternative Healing Solutions

"The Intuitive Mind is a sacred gift, the rational mind, a loyal servant. Our society has honored the servant and forgotten the gift."
—ALBERT EINSTEIN

Significant research is being done in the field of alternative healing. An office has been established at the National Institute of Health, with funding dedicated to determine why and how this phenomena is taking off. In the U.S. alone, 15 billion dollars is spent annually on herbs, vitamins, nutritional products, and medical schools now offer classes in alternative healing. We are making progress.

The Benefits of Alternative Healing Methods

To sum up, here are eight compelling reasons to pursue alternative healing options:

1. Physical awareness is intensified.
2. Emotional, mental, and spiritual issues are addressed simultaneously.
3. Intuition becomes clearer.
4. Heightened body awareness makes prevention and self-care easier.
5. The body is restored to health naturally, without reliance on drugs.
6. You get smarter—even at the cellular level.
7. You experience more compassion and love, because it is from this place healing occurs.
8. You ultimately learn how to activate a healing state on your own, without assistance.

I remember when I first began studying CranioSacral therapy with John Upledger, D.O., F.A.A.O., a physician and passionate CranioSacral researcher at the University of Michigan. He explained to us, "I attempted to teach this technique to my colleagues. When I showed them the simple manipulations on the cranial bones, they weren't interested." Dr. Upledger was forced to take the technique to hands-on practitioners—physical therapists, chiropractors, dentists, and occupational and massage therapists.

Alternative healing and traditional medicine are still in different camps, but the two are rapidly bridging the gap by sharing their wealth of knowledge. Integrative medicine, which combines the best high-tech Western medicine with alternative approaches, is now being offered at an ever-increasing number of hospitals and medical centers.

I heartily recommend alternative techniques for all stress-related conditions. Researchers agree that the majority of illness is influenced by stress. If you don't have a serious health condition now, these techniques can prevent trouble in the future. If you're flirting with a burnout, have been under pressure, or are on the edge of some type of breakdown, these therapies are possible alternatives to pharmaceutical solutions. The idea is to bring the body back naturally to a balanced healing state.

I've personally experienced each of the techniques in this chapter and find that, in combination, they help (1) create a calmer presence, (2) foster greater self-awareness, and (3) boost intuition. Several body systems are addressed, and I fully expect that you'll find some better suited to your needs than others. As you work with each technique, you'll become better educated on how to listen to your body through a personally tailored and eclectic approach.

To begin, let's explore the healing recipe for a CALM life:

- C is for Chiropractic and CranioSacral Therapy.
- A is for Acupuncture and the Alexander Technique.
- L is for Lomilomi Massage and Lymph Drainage Therapy.
- M is for Acupressure, Deep Tissue and Swedish Massage.

Each technique is designed to balance the body through touch or movement, or a combination of both.

C is for Chiropractic and CranioSacral Therapy

Chiropractic Medicine

Chiropractic treatments are now considered pretty much mainstream and are covered by a number of health plans. Chiropractic care combined with other alternative therapies offers a well-balanced approach to health. It addresses the central nervous system by aligning the bones, and is based on the theory that the health of the entire body is connected to the condition of the spine. If bones are not aligned properly, the nerve centers that feed various organs and systems (i.e., digestive, respiratory, etc.) can't supply the blood and oxygen needed for optimal health. Initial visits can last up to an hour and generally include X-rays. After that, adjustments usually take from 10 to 30 minutes.

Indications: Musculoskeletal disorders respond well, including whiplash, low back pain, sprain or strain, arthritic conditions, sciatica, and neck problems. Known as organic conditions, headaches, high blood pressure, nervous disorders, and migraines also frequently respond to chiropractic care.

Cost: $35–75 per visit; initial office visit is usually double that amount.

CranioSacral Therapy

This unique therapy addresses the hydraulic system that encloses the brain, spinal cord, cerebrospinal fluid, cranial bones, sacrum, and dural membrane. Through gentle manipulations and a light touch, tensions and blocks are released from this central core of the body that create imbalance, dysfunction, and fatigue. Using a process called "unwinding," advanced CST practitioners allow the body to release specific trauma by recreating the body's position when the injury occurred. This can happen spontaneously if the trauma is ready to be corrected and the practitioner follows the CranioSacral rhythm. It's no surprise that blocks arising from emotional or physical trauma "hide out" in this central core. When left unaddressed, they become like rocks in a stream, impeding our life force and full use of sensory faculties. Once released, the body's energy and vitality are restored and awareness is heightened. This is an effective and spiritual approach to healing the body. Treatments take from one to two hours.

Indications: Several conditions can benefit from CST: headaches, nervous problems, TMJ, back pain, ear and eye disorders, depression, learning disabilities, chronic fatigue syndrome, and hyperactivity.

Cost: $75–$125 per hour.

A is for Acupuncture and the Alexander Technique

Acupuncture

This well-known Eastern technique uses needles to open up the meridians of the body. These meridians are energy channels that allow the life forced called "chi" to activate and energize us. Vital people have an abundance of this life force pulsing throughout their system. Acupuncturists make diagnoses by listening to the pulses in the wrists, noting the color of the tongue, and assessing symptoms. They then determine which points they will stimulate with extremely thin (almost hair-like) acupuncture needles. (Those who normally turn pale at the sight of a syringe needn't worry—this is *not* like getting an injection.) Sometimes a small battery-powered electrical device is used to provide more stimulation to open up blocked energy centers. Another enhancement is *moxabustion*. In this process a cigar-shaped stick made of Chinese mugwort is ignited and used as a heat source to stimulate the needles, activating the chi at various points.

Indications: Pain, organ imbalances, headaches, allergies, asthma, back problems, stress, nervous conditions, insomnia, impotency, frozen shoulder and joint problems. Treatments usually take 30–60 minutes, and are both relaxing and revitalizing.

Cost: $65–$125 per treatment.

Alexander Technique

Frederick Matthias Alexander was an aspiring actor with a promising career when he developed vocal difficulties. His doctors didn't have a solution, so he began observing his neck and head in the mirror while speaking. He concluded that faulty postural habits were creating his vocal dysfunction. After healing his own voice, he helped others alter incorrect or inefficient physical habits that were causing stress and fatigue.

The Alexander Technique recognizes the maintenance of the neck muscles and position of the head as primary requirements for efficient use of the body. Through a series of lessons to improve one's awareness of movement patterns, this approach addresses unconscious misuse of the body in performing everyday tasks. Relaxation techniques and simple exercises to retrain the muscles are used to improve posture.

Indications: Popular among professional athletes, musicians, dancers, and actors. This technique reduces tension and stress in everyday activities, improves coordination and self-awareness, and also reduces various types of chronic pain.

Cost: $35–85 per session, usually one hour. Group classes are less expensive.

L is for Lomilomi Massage and Lymph Drainage Therapy

Lomilomi Massage

"Auntie" Margaret Machado learned this technique exclusively for Hawaiian royalty and shared it with the rest of the healing world. A relaxing and invigorating form of Hawaiian massage steeped in ancient tradition, it breaks up muscle spasms with a series of movements of the hands, forearms, and elbows. The overall effect is very nurturing, touching the heart through the practitioner's hands. Sessions incorporate physical and spiritual aspects of healing, allowing the body to release stress and toxins.

Indications: Beneficial for musculoskeletal disorders, pregnancy, muscle tension, and stress relief. This technique's nurturing quality helps heal emotional loss and grief.

Cost: $65–$95 per hour. 75–90 minute sessions are recommended.

Lymph Drainage Therapy

You might call the lymph system the body's "garbage disposal." This "wonder fluid" runs throughout the body wherever there is blood. Responsible for detoxification of the tissues, it is also the pathway of cellular immunity for B-cells and T-cells. Whether we're fighting cancer or the common cold, it is the lymph system's effectiveness that bolsters immunity and fights infection. This method, developed by Bruno Chikly, M.D., effectively stimulates the lymphatic flow, opening up the lymph system of those with chronic edema and autoimmune disease. When lymph isn't moving efficiently, our body becomes toxic and can produce mental, physical, and emotional imbalances. In an LDT session, selected points are stimulated, moving stagnant lymph and inflation by increasing lymph circulation through the body. One should drink plenty of water before and after a session to maximize the cleansing effect. Sessions are relaxing and regenerating, and stimulate the parasympathetic function.

Indications: Inflammatory disorders such as bronchitis, sinusitis, arthritis, acne, eczema, and chronic fatigue syndrome; it also helps depression and hyperactivity syndrome.

Cost: $60–150 per session.

All massage stimulates the parasympathetic function of the body. In his book, *Silent Waves, Theory and Practice of Lymph Drainage Therapy*, Dr. Bruno Chikly points out that the parasympathetic function is generally most active during sleep and deep relaxation states, and that its function is to conserve and help restore body energy, regenerating injured tissues.

Here are some of the benefits of Lymph Drainage Therapy listed in Dr. Chikly's book:

- Stimulates immune functions
- Decreases heart rate
- Decreases respiratory rate
- Decreases blood pressure
- Increases blood flow to skin
- Increases blood sugar level
- Increases gastrointestinal motility and kidney function
- Increases digestive gland function
- Increases bronchial gland function
- Increases salivary gland function

M is for Acupressure, Deep Tissue, and Swedish Massage

Acupressure Massage

This treatment uses the same principle of activating energy centers and meridian points as acupuncture, but stimulation occurs through touch rather than the piercing of the skin. (This is great for those who get white knuckles even at the *thought* of a needle!)

Muscular tension accumulates around acupressure points, which causes muscle groups to contract and block the flow of vital life force throughout the body.

Indications: Menstrual problems, migraine headaches, insomnia, digestive disorders, backaches, and muscular pain are some of the maladies that respond well to this treatment.

Cost: $65–$95 per hour session.

Deep Tissue Massage

Although this isn't for the "faint of heart" this level of massage is ideal for many people who need chronic kinks worked out of their bodies. The practitioners' focus is on muscles and fascia, the webbed tissue that keeps us toned and solid. Using elbows, forearms and heavy pressure, the blocks are released that impede proper function.

Deeper memories of past emotional traumas can be accessed in these parts of the body. Sometimes this type of massage can be painful in the moment, and even for a day or so afterwards, but the long term benefits are worth it. The results are you feel freer than you've felt in a long time, the range of motion in the joints is greater, and a renewed sense of energy.

Indications: Chronic tension in back, neck, shoulders, stiff joints, and fatigue. Athletes love this type of bodywork to keep muscles toned and healthy to resist or heal from injury.

Cost: $75-$135 per hour.

Swedish Massage

One of the most popular massage techniques, commonly offered in health clubs and spas, it includes a variety of strokes: kneading, shaking, light percussion, and cross-friction, addressing the entire body. This approach is designed to wake up or energize the body through increased circulation. Benefits include relief for sore muscles, improved circulation, reduced swelling, and overall relaxation. An added bonus is a mood lift, because Swedish massage stimulates endorphins.

Indications: Fatigue, depression, sore muscles, pregnancy, headaches, stiff necks, back and shoulder pain, fluid retention, and insomnia.

Cost: $50–$125 per hour.

Experience really counts here. Most massage therapists start with Swedish and then add other techniques as they gain experience.

The Importance of Energy Alignment

When we visit a practitioner, it's vital that we feel relaxed in his or her presence. Even if someone comes highly recommended, if you don't feel completely comfortable, then you need to find another source. Your well-being should be a practitioner's top priority, and their energy should be harmonious with yours as they work to open up your blocks and energy imbalances. Once that is established, miracles can occur.

When we feel out of balance, we're at a disadvantage because in times of vulnerability we tend to lose our normal sense of discernment and clarity. All too often we grant health practitioners too much power, which can be dangerous if we happen across someone unscrupulous. Except in a medical emergency, we should never turn our entire well-being over to the care of someone else. It is not the job of any one doctor or healthcare practitioner to restore and heal us. *That is our job.* We must select our experts carefully, and take responsibility for our choice of treatments.

If someone recommends a treatment that strikes us as absurd—it probably is. And try to avoid prescriptions that create more toxins in the body and an even greater need for alternative healing. In addition to good common sense, here are a few guidelines.

Ten Things to Look for in an Alternative Healing Practitioner

1. Positive, uplifting energy and presence
2. Understanding, easy to relate to
3. Good communicator
4. Provides professional materials and literature
5. Provides a pleasant, clean environment
6. Focuses on you and your specific needs
7. Considerate of your time
8. May offer—but doesn't push—additional products or services
9. Willing to accommodate you in a crisis
10. Credentials and current licenses on display

If fees are higher than average, services should be exceptional and customized. Lower than average fees may reflect a sacrifice in one or more of the areas listed above.

Cautionary Tales

Having been both a patient and a practitioner for years, I've heard a lot of stories and have a few of my own. Here are a couple of cautionary tales to assist you in making wise choices.

Trust Your Instincts, Not a Doctor's Ego

One of my experiences occurred after a spiritual retreat in England. The lessons I learned that summer were unexpected and profound. My body felt out of sorts. I felt so vulnerable that I sought out someone new to help me. My first choice was a chiropractor who was also an acupuncturist. On my initial visit, he seemed extremely confident and boasted about the uniqueness of his method. He claimed he could cure the pain in my neck, still stressed from whiplash injuries. He convinced me that I needed adjustments *twice a week*. This was about six sessions more per month than I'd had in the past. But this man was so convincing that I followed his advice—in spite of nagging doubts.

Within a short time I experienced the worst pain I'd ever known: migraine-like headaches, lower back pain, and an overall sense of disorientation. Finally I realized this practitioner was more interested in advancing his business (and his bank account) than in serving my needs.

Knowing When to Move On

Another doctor of energy medicine was phenomenal. In spite of my regular self-care regime, I was fatigued and couldn't seem to find relief. Because I was building my speaking career while maintaining a private practice, I needed extra support.

From the very beginning I had incredible rapport with this doctor. I felt like I could handle anything, knowing I had this clearing, healing energy to balance me. I was so pleased, in fact, that I became a big fan.

After a couple years, however, I began to notice signs of burnout in this hardworking doctor. Within weeks this doctor had a bizarre seizure and was rushed to the hospital by paramedics. Instead of taking time off and getting back in balance, this doctor kept seeing clients and pushing to the limit.

Soon I began to feel that I was the healer and the doctor was the recipient. I realized that I shouldn't be spending my time and money this way. It was time for me to acknowledge that our work together was complete.

There are still those who think anything outside the realm of traditional medicine is primitive or downright flaky. The truth is, we need both the practical and the magical to maintain a healthy mind and body. I certainly don't recommend that you stop seeing your medical doctor. I'm just suggesting that if you aren't getting the results you want, and medical tests aren't shedding enough light on your condition, it might be time to try the alternative approach. But before you take a leap, read, learn, and open your mind. You deserve to feel connected, whole, and balanced to enjoy every day of your life to the fullest.

CHAPTER TEN

Spiritual Healing Solutions

"One moon dispels the darkness of the heav-
ens. Similarly, one soul who is trained to know
God, a soul in whom there is true devotion,
sincere seeking, and intensity will dispel the
spiritual darkness of others wherever they will
go."

—PARMAHANSA YOGANANDA

As I mentioned in the last chapter, alternative healing opens us up to greater awareness, intuition, and calming
energy. For many it's a welcomed relief to tune in to life at
a deeper level. However, the more open and compassion-
ate you become, the more awareness you need to maintain
this inner peace.

Spiritual Protection

As open and peaceful vessels of light in a sometimes dark and chaotic world, we may find ourselves feeling vulnerable. When we're standing up to serve humankind's highest good, we shouldn't have to live in a state of worry. Protection, in the sense I'm using it here, is an ancient wisdom and has nothing to do with the guys in *The Sopranos*. When warriors of old went into battle, they often carried a talisman for protection. A St. Christopher medal for Catholics is another example. And American Indians wear beautiful stones to complement various medicines.

One of my clients used to buy a lot of Indian jewelry. After years of searching, finally she came across a grizzly claw to wear as a pendant. Since she had a strong belief in Native American animal medicines, she felt a great sense of protection in this magical ornament.

A few years back I began wearing a Personal Rejuvenizer, a pendant with properties to protect from electromagnetic fields (EMFs). Before wearing this pendant I couldn't work on my computer for more than 60–90 minutes at a stretch. I'd have problems with eyestrain, headaches, and fatigue. I also caught the common cold or flu repeatedly. When I then learned about EMFs and how they influence the energy field, which does affect immunity, I knew I was one who needed this special protection. The writing of this book wouldn't have been possible without my Rejuvenizer, and I can do the extended travel my profession requires without getting sick. I'm grateful to Dr. Phyllis Light from Austin, Texas, the creator of the Personal Rejuvenizer. Her gifts as a telepathic healer specializing in subtle energy fields are the cornerstone of this unique protective device.

Certain clothes can also evoke feelings of power. A few famous athletes have even been rumored to wear something lacy under their uniforms during championship games, but I'm not suggesting anything that exotic. Cloaks worn by holy men and "power suits" donned by today's corporate warriors show the significance of our attire. I've purchased my share of "power" outfits over the years. One I recall was a casual beige summer pantsuit that I got before meeting the Dalai Lama. At that event we performed an empowerment for Shakyamuni Buddha, and my special outfit still makes me feel protected and empowered.

We can also place a specific intention in objects to protect us in special ways. People who are attracted to crystals and minerals might place these objects in their home, office, or car to protect their environment. The way I look at protection is that it must come from a higher level. I frequently ask God for the protection I need to complete projects or attend events where I know my energy will be challenged.

How do we access this protection? First of all, prayer is the greatest protector of all for those who are able to humble themselves. Second, we can ask in our meditations how we can be shielded, and then strengthen that protection in ourselves. Third, we can simply ask. *Seek and ye shall find.*

In some of my Day of Healing seminars, I offer a guided meditation where I ask people to call up their special protection, and afterward I invite participants to share their experiences. Some people see glorious visualizations that they continue to call upon. One person saw himself sheltered by a pair of cupped hands that emitted a swirl of energy. Another envisioned a translucent bubble that was flexible and iridescent, reflecting a rainbow of colors. This bubble surrounded her and pushed all negative energy away. Another woman pictured herself enveloped in a flame of red, gold, and white. Still others saw a purple or violet flame and felt a crackling presence that evaporated anything negative that drew near.

The Gift of Clairvoyance

The gift of sight is called clairvoyance, and those who see angels and energy fields called "auras" have this special talent. One of the world's best-known clairvoyants was an American named Edgar Cayce. When people came to him seeking relief from illness, he could go into a trance and locate the origin of the disease. He is said to have cured people whom doctors had failed. Word of his gift spread and he eventually had to get an unlisted number because people were constantly calling him. If strangers came to him in anger, he would see their rage before they approached, and he requested that they return when their emotions were under control. This is the way he protected himself, and you can too!

Clairvoyance can come from inner sight rather than external visions or auras. My initial sense of protection was signaled by a rush of energy through the central core of my body. For me, the spinal column became activated— more alive and more energized. My protection came in the form of energy that would originate at the top of my head, streaming in from above, healing me.

This special gift—this sense of protection—only comes from expanding one's inner sight and inner gifts, and usually develops with the practice of meditation. I encourage people to begin regular meditation and participate in healing seminars or church services. If the universe seems to deliver up a special healer, pay attention. Masters like the Dalai Lama can walk into a room and emanate a calming presence. Invisible boulders arise and are released. That is what a healer does—he or she helps to lift obstacles and set the person free. The more we develop our protection, faith, and inner strength, the more we encourage our own calming presence. Borrow from those who are where *you* want to be, in an effort to reach that special place *you* need to go.

Inner Chaos and Invisible Boulders

Inner chaos often stems from painful accumulations of belief systems from the past. When we have oversized emotional reactions to situations, the past is affecting the present. The 80/20 theory works here to describe these responses: 20 percent of my reaction is to the current situation and 80 percent is from past situations. When we reinforce these ideas long enough, they eventually take on the psychic weight of an invisible boulder.

I came upon the "boulder theory" while working as a group facilitator. One team member kept shifting her position about the duties she was willing to take on. Finally, after she accepted a position of responsibility, then declined it, and then she asked for more responsibility, I turned down her offer. As the facilitator I had to note her inconsistency. When I didn't award her the position, an invisible boulder developed between us. Communication ceased, blocked by this impenetrable wall.

When incidents like this occur in my life, I always assess my actions, my intentions, and my attitude. I take partial responsibility for creating the boulder because relationships are never one-sided. People act and react to pebbles, boulders, walls, and cold shoulders. They respond much better to openness, warmth, cooperation, and appreciation. That's why, when our mind is clear and our thoughts are positive, we feel we are in "the zone" and attract only good. If I experience anything less, I know it's time to take a look at *me*. And I'd better, because that's what I teach!

I believe a major key to success is self-knowledge. I wish more employers would address self-knowledge and communication/behavior-style programs rather than focusing so much on customer service and bottom-line sales skills.

Dismantling the Boulders

When invisible boulders arise in my life, I like to open communications with the other person, *once I'm certain that I'm going forth with openness and a kind heart.* I might say, "I notice that after such-and-such happened we haven't been able to talk. Are you willing to discuss the situation to clear the air and maybe find a solution?" This opener helps us confront the problem and heal it head-on.

EXERCISE: Inner Boulder Clearing

If you notice that you keep having "boulder situations" with different people, then you might want to try what I humbly call an "inner boulder clearing."

Answer the following question as honestly as possible: Which of your relationships are blocked by "invisible boulders"—caused by resentments, disappointments, jealousy, or ill wishes?

1. _____

2. _____

3. _____

4. _____

5. _____

6. _____

7. _____

8. _____

9. _____

10. _____

Now that you've listed your troubled relationships, create four columns on a blank sheet of paper, as follows:

Name of Person	Incident	Date of Occurrence	Plan of Action
1.			
2.			
3.			
4.			
5.			
6.			
7.			
8.			
9.			
10.			

Now comes the good part. Doing this exercise will help you release or *blow apart* this boulder so you're no longer burdened by its weight. Here are a few examples to get you started:

Name of Person	Incident	Date of Occurrence	Plan of Action
1. Penny	In the last years of our relationship, she pretended to be my friend, yet revealed to others what I told her in confidence. Finally she ended our friendship with a Dear Jane letter.	Five years ago	Prayer, forgiveness, and finding something to be grateful for. I will pray for Penny's good fortune, forgive her for hurting me, and I'll write a letter–but not necessarily mail it–expressing my forgiveness and gratitude for the good times we shared.
2. Jill	Under the pretense of being helpful, she told me things about myself that were hurtful. Some of her observations were true, but her words were needlessly cruel; there was nothing constructive about the delivery.	Three mo. ago	My plan is to talk to friends to release my sadness and grief. In my thoughts I'll wish Jill well and try to let go of my negative energy (i.e., that Plymouth Rock–sized boulder!) I'll accept the shift and confide in her less.
3. The unofficial photographer of the family, one of my father's best friends	He always ignored me as a child. When he took pictures at family events, he never photographed me. It was almost as if I didn't exist.	More than 30 years ago	I carried out my plan of action, which was to visit him and pray for a miracle. My father's best friend was emotional in my presence and commented on how well I looked. The best part was seeing him in tears after I said good-bye and went back to say "I love you." I knew then the boulder was gone.

*Resentment is a waste—it's like swallowing
poison, hoping the other person will die. As we
seethe about how "they done me wrong,"
feeling worse with each recollection, the other
person is free as a bird, kicking up his heels,
having fun.*

This is a great exercise for detecting patterns in our relationships with others, and determining which ones are the "heavies." Pain is part of life, people do let us down, and everyone has "stuff." Life will sometimes deliver our dreams to others while we stand there empty-handed, wondering what went wrong. Maybe our best friend gets the job, or the guy we had our heart set on. *Pain happens, but misery is optional.* Misery is focusing on the pain over and over; misery is self-inflicted pain. Focus on your pain, feed it, fan its flames, and it will morph into The Greatest Pain of All Time.

I knew a woman who constantly complained about her husband. Nothing he did seemed to please her and his idiosyncrasies were a constant source of irritation. The last few times I saw her, the joyful glow of earlier days was gone. Not only was her expression troubled, but she sighed deeply with any reference to her marriage.

The Boulder-Clearing Process takes more than writing a list with four columns

To clear most boulders, it's best to confront the person involved—either by phone or in person. With advances in technology, it's easy to e-mail our lives away. Where something as major as a boulder is concerned, it's best to use electronic communication only as a last resort. When you want to clear the air of these "heavies," you need an exchange of personal energy to resolve old wounds and conflicts.

Unless a disease is revealed, it cannot be healed

The boulders in your life can progress over time from dis-ease to continually reinforced disease. When I think of the cancer epidemic in our society, I think of unresolved inner boulders, which can create lumps, bumps, and tumors in the body.

Reframe Yourself

Reframing is one of the best ways to keep sane during difficult times. It is a thought process that uses your own power of visualization to shape an old reality into a new perspective. We need to reframe something when a situation makes us feel defeated. Reframing these troublesome incidents can free us from constant replays, which places a heavy load on our hearts. Once that burden is uncovered and explored, we can find a source of power in our wounds, mistakes, and lost opportunities. One of my first teachers used to say "*Uncover, discover, discard.*" The freedom is in the discard.

Something that haunted me for years was missing my favorite grandmother's funeral. At the time of her death, the family decided it wasn't necessary to fly me back to Michigan for the service. But when the day arrived, I couldn't stop thinking about Grandma, about how wonderful she was and what gifts she'd given me. She was a sharp dresser, classy, musically talented, kind to others, a great cook, and she loved children. When I called home,

I was told my mother had refused to cry at the funeral. Instead she had grabbed my cousin's hand and squeezed it, silently determined not to "break down." When I heard this I wept for hours. I was overwhelmed with emotion and felt yet again that I was the emotional faucet for the family, the designated griever.

Years later, as I repeatedly witnessed the healing aspects of funerals, I felt deep regret that I didn't just fly myself back for my grandmother's service. However tardy, I knew I needed some closure on Grandma's passing.

The opportunity to reframe this missed funeral came when I attended a weekend retreat. The workshop leader decided to stage a mock funeral, a ceremony where we could grieve the loss of a behavior we wanted to stop or a person we needed to let go of. I decided this was the time to hold my own private funeral for my grandmother. I cried over my loss, told people how great she was, and just spent the rest of the afternoon in quiet reflection. This reframing of a lost opportunity freed my energy and finally put my grief to rest. I discarded this circumstance that had burdened me for years. It was all I needed to free up my soul.

Sometimes we need to be creative in reframing an event. There won't always be a class or workshop to provide the perfect opportunity. This is where journaling can offer a great release. Where else can you verbally air your laundry—completely uncensored? If you have pain in your life leftover from childhood, teenage years, or unexpected life events, you can walk around with chronic fatigue from all these unresolved conflicts. If you reframe old traumas one by one, discarding them from your psyche, you can lighten up your life and free yourself from inner chaos, which is how *all* turmoil begins. If we wonder why the world is so chaotic these days, it's because most people keep racing through life, creating more disordered patterns, in an endless vicious circle. By learning to uncover, discover, and discard, we can put down our burdens and experience the joy of being free.

CHAPTER ELEVEN

Restore, Relax, Renew

"A mind too active is no mind at all."
—THEODORE ROETHKE

The fast-paced chaos most of us are experiencing causes us to become stressed out and eventually jaded. When we're jaded, we lose touch with our body and soul. Alternative healing helps us update our hard drive so we can keep being a productive human-*doing*. Spiritual healing frees up the heaviness in our soul, and certain self-care solutions keep our life in balance by connecting us to our human-*being*.

One of my mentors, an award-winning speaker, regales audiences with tales of her fast-track days. During her early years she worked incredibly hard, scheduling every minute for optimal productivity. Now she admits that after a few years at breakneck speed, she began to feel like a robot. Reading through her daily agenda of sales calls, speaking engagements, and staff meetings, she jokes that she even used to schedule in time for lovemaking with her husband. She would recite in a robotic voice: "10:00–10:20—make love with Larry. Oops! He's late—gotta start without him!"

Audiences always roar with laughter when she tells this story. My friend touches a nerve in almost everyone, because she's kidding on the square. Most of us know at some level that there's a certain *joie de vivre* that gets lost in the shuffle when we over-schedule ourselves. But pressures mount, and we do what we feel we have to do. When we finally take a breather from the robot track and take time to restore ourselves, we become more authentic. By allowing time for human-*being* without human-*doing*, we can rediscover our own inner rhythms of productivity and creativity, and our instincts about what's right for *us*.

Here are seven ways you can use your physical senses to nurture your body, mind, and soul:

1. Earthwalking

What's the difference between normal walking and Earthwalking? A Kucchina Indian woman once explained to me that the Earth is our mother and our friend because it has restorative powers and transmutation powers. Those who can consciously engage these powers are called shamans. One of their prescriptions for encouraging a blissful-wise-healing state is Earthwalking. This simply means walking barefoot, mindful of where we step as we seek out the Earth's energies to rebalance us, consciously releasing negative energies and anxieties.

To engage in this practice, simply visualize drain-like openings on the bottoms of your feet, then imagine pulling out the stopper and allowing your negative emotions—anger, jealousy, anxiety, hostility, turmoil—to pour out of your body, through the feet and into the ground. Sometimes I use the analogy of a camera lens that adjusts according to the available light. Think of the imaginary openings on your soles as apertures, replacing negative energy with the healing energy of the Earth.

The beach or a grassy meadow is an ideal place to Earthwalk, but any field or trail will do. And as my wise Indian friend likes to say, "Smoother surfaces are easier on tender feet."

If you can't or don't wish to experience Earth's energy through your feet, you can take it in through your senses. Breathe in the fresh air, listen to the sounds of nature, and notice the wind or calm in the air. Attune your senses to the outdoors where Mother Nature is doing her thing— and will help us do ours if we allow her.

2. Water Power

Water rules our planet. Our bodies are 76% water. Without it, we quickly die. A book titled *Your Body's Many Cries for Water* by Fereydoon Batmanghelidj documents an array of afflictions including back problems, arthritis, heart disease and hormone imbalances that can be reversed by keeping the body properly hydrated. The importance of drinking water (roughly two quarts a day), cannot be stressed enough. Water washes and nourishes our bodies from the inside out. Try drinking an extra quart of water one day a week, and see if you notice the difference.

Dehydration will slow your metabolism, and can cause fatigue and even depression. People sometimes mistake the thirst mechanism for hunger. The next time you're hungry, try drinking a 16-ounce glass of water. This has been a dieter's secret for years. The more water you drink, the less food you'll crave. And don't worry about water retention. The body hoards water when it gets *too little*, and discards it when it gets enough.

And don't think other liquids will replace the need for H_2O. Caffeine and alcohol have a mild diuretic effect. So if you indulge, become a two-fisted drinker: Down some extra water for each glass of wine or cup of coffee. (Note: If your water intake is currently low, it's best to increase it gradually, adding a glass or two a day until you reach eight.)

What do swimming pools, Jacuzzis, oceans, rivers, and streams all have in common? These various sources of water all have the ability to clear and restore the body. Even if we don't immerse ourselves in water, we feel better just being in the presence of a lovely river, lake, or stream. And we benefit from the positive effect of negative ions whenever we take a shower or walk by the ocean. When I don't have the time to seek out nature's venues, I create my own private wet zone by filling a tub with scented bath salts. A salt soak at the end of the day is a wonderful way to restore oneself and prepare the body for a good night's sleep. Dead Sea salts, rich in restorative minerals, are the most powerful and worth the extra cost. *Masada* makes a good product, *Kerstin Florian* salts are very potent, and *Batherapy* is a longtime favorite. *Masada* and *Batherapy* are available at most health food stores.

When traveling on a long flight or if you've been out in a large crowd and feel depleted, try taking a quick shower using Salt Suds by Origins for the time-management version of a salt soak. This formula contains sea salts and essential oils to relax and purify your body.

3. Fire Power

Have you ever noticed how relaxed you feel after sitting in a sauna or lazing around a roaring fire? Fire is a powerful tool for clearing and freeing the mind; the whole premise of *Ashtanga* Yoga is to stoke the inner fire. A bonfire on the beach is especially healing because you have the essence of water and fire combined. But if a day (or night) at the shore is a dream out of reach, you can still experience the healing powers of fire from the sun. Just a half hour or so of sunbathing can soothe and heal body and mind. And don't let a little sweat bother you; it's an effective way to rid yourself of toxins and tension. Just be sure, especially if you're fair-skinned, to slather on the sunscreen—and avoid the burning rays in the middle of the day. If you don't have a fireplace, another way to access fire power is to burn candles. The glow of candlelight always brings a sort of "aahhh" quality to enhance relaxation.

4. Oil Power

The power of aromatherapy is another vehicle for renewal. The ancient Egyptians used essential oils to heal and protect them from the desert sun. Today we are fortunate to have so many fine brands of these near-magical potions. Clary sage clears the mind and lifts the spirits. Lavender calms and soothes. Rose is relaxing and opens the heart. Rosemary stimulates circulation and energizes. Eucalyptus helps us breathe. Bergamot minimizes depression and helps combat PMS. Lemon is cleansing and clearing. Blue Tansy is paradise in a formula blended with other oils. In the United States, *Aveda* has marketed essential oils and aromatherapy products since the '80s. England has high-grade suppliers because they have used essential oils in medical clinics for decades. Single oils are potent and powerful, but blended oils are like perfume with performance. They produce a richer, more complex smell and magnify the impact.

If the idea of wearing oils isn't appealing, you can diffuse essential oils into the air and breathe in the fragrance. A candle made with essential oils is also helpful if it is lit nearby. If oils in any form don't work for you, incense or room fragrance can deliver aromas to help you feel balanced and restored. A great incense line is *Escential Essences*, and my two favorites are called Purification and Prosperity. A fantastic home fragrance line is *Thymes Limited*, out of Minneapolis. Bath gels and soaps can also deliver essential oil power. *Origins* Clean Comfort makes a soothing bath wash with chamomile, rosemary, petigrain, and sage.

5. Inner Circle Power

Nothing beats the power of friendship. It's essential to our well-being to have like-minded friends who will support us and help us grow, and whom we can help in return. Twelve-step programs are a great place to take your emotional baggage if an addiction pattern is present or if family alcoholism is an issue. Al-Anon is the family program associated with Alcoholics Anonymous, and I've never seen such troopers. These people will stand by you and get you back on track no matter how tough your situation.

Churches, too, are a fortress of spiritual development and companionship. I've been to some that offer such extensive classes that they're almost like a junior college and church all rolled into one. You'll know you're in the right place when you find yourself among kindred spirits. Another great format for those in the creative arts (or those who aspire to be) are support groups like Artist's Way. Julia Cameron's work is tailored to clear out the chaos so you can expand your horizons and creativity. HMOs and hospices offer support groups for those facing illness or loss, which is when we most need inner-circle power. Whenever you find yourself struggling with chaos and internal or external difficulties, this is the time to turn to others. You'll find a sense of calm in togetherness.

6. Family Power

Nothing compares to time with family. There is a history that magically binds us together when we allow the good times to prevail. If you think you come from a dysfunctional-beyond-belief family, cultivate one person in your clan whom you can talk to when you need more than a friend. Just having the same parents or grandparents gives us a commonality we can't share with the outside world. Family members will usually be aware of both our strengths and weaknesses, and the fact they stick by and love us in spite of it all, is restorative and reassuring.

I have a favorite Aunt from childhood who now lives in Florida. When I was growing up people always compared me to her. Our common link is our gift of gab and a love for my dad. When we talk about family, so much gets healed. We share a common perspective and family resemblance. We can laugh till we cry and cry until we laugh. In one hour we can rehash the decades, for we enjoy a special, richly textured intimacy.

7. Breath Power

Here is the one thing in your life you can always control—your breathing. The rate, the depth, the sound, and the location are all within your control. Through Yoga I have learned to take deep Yogic breaths. They have a restorative effect. You constrict your throat and extend the breath by lengthening the time spent breathing in and out. This throat constriction creates a sort of Darth Vader–like sound that further helps focus your mind on just one thing: the breath you are taking now. Deep diaphragmic breaths slow down the brain, oxygenate the body, and create a sense of total relaxation.

When I'm highly stressed I sometimes have trouble getting to sleep. I've learned to coax myself into a state of sleep-inducing relaxation with these deep-breathing techniques. When I focus on lengthening each breath, the narrowing throat sound eases my worries away. Thank you, God, for this built-in stress-reducing tool; it's so much better than turning to one of our not-so-healthy habits. (Parents of young children whose sleep is often interrupted will find this tool especially helpful.)

Light Breathing

Here's a quick breathing exercise you can do anywhere. It helps to close your eyes (unless you're behind the wheel), and then visualize your breath as a radiant light filling your body. See the light/breath entering your mouth and spilling down your throat. As the light uses the spine to direct its way through the central core of the body, feel yourself let go and experience a sense of renewal. The more breaths you take, the lighter you feel, and the more energized you become. Continue until you feel completely filled with light from within. Then enjoy this light moment. As you open your eyes, look into a mirror. See if you don't shine a little brighter!

Clearing Power

Sometimes "clearing" can occur immediately after an Earthwalk or a relaxing salt soak, but other times it's not so easy. When we carry resentments and allow anger to rule us, we become heavy from the chaos in our minds and bodies. Clearing ourselves is a way of achieving a calmer state. I often ask people during workshops, "Where do you live?" They usually reply with a geographic location. After I hear several answers, I say, "No, you all live one place—within your own skin." How clean is that house, the house within? As someone who works with energy, I find it will sometimes take days to clear myself from the stress of a heavy workload. I then have to remind myself that I am clearing my "house" of negative energy, so I just keep breathing, walking, oiling, soaking, sunning, and connecting with my inner circle of friends and family, until I'm ready to roar again.

We actually impede our progress when we overexert our bodies and get burned out just to achieve some mighty ambition. No glory is worth it if we destroy our health in the process.

C-a-n-c-e-r. Have I got your attention? Many cancers might be prevented if people would take time out to share their burdens in the sanctuary of a support group instead of smoking or drinking themselves into the ER. Ignoring aches and pains or masking them with medications can allow cancer to get a foothold at the cellular level. A friend of mine, a wonderful motivational speaker, developed a cancer of the blood that was difficult to detect. He was an expert on time management and gave seminars around the country. But he forgot to keep his own life in balance and raced his engines on high for too long. I love this guy and felt so sad that at 57, he hadn't learned how to slow down and nurture himself.

Another example to learn from was an overcommitted father and husband who worked himself into a state of poor health. He needed a kidney transplant at the age of 42, but refused to follow his doctors' instructions during the healing process. Within a year he was on crutches and in need of one, if not two, hip replacements. He wasn't able to benefit fully from 21st century medicine because he failed to do his part in restoring his health. Is this accomplishment?

According to Taoist philosophy, our every movement results from the force that directs and orchestrates life. The master is one who yields to this force and allows events to occur, knowing that the master's task is to stay composed and clear. In this clear state of mind and body we can react with purpose and pleasure, no matter what the circumstance.

Several stories have been told about people who faced tragedy yet possessed a clear sense of purpose and confidence, even in the midst of grave danger. This is how the Taoist master lives. In the aftermath of tragedy, we have to take each day and allow the forces to play out without engaging all our projections of fear and doubt. We all have deep emotional patterns and fears we must face. Any tragedy is a wake-up call forcing us to live at a higher level if we want to achieve purpose and pleasure during times of danger and uncertainty. Who ever said life was a sure thing? But as long as you are alive, your inner house is certain, for it is where you live.

How do you change the world? One person at a time.

CHAPTER TWELVE

The Power of Prayer

"All you need to do to receive guidance is to ask for it and then listen."

—SANAYA ROMAN

If you don't think prayer can provide peace, think for a moment about the late Mother Teresa. If you don't believe prayer gives you strength to overcome adversity, remember Rose Kennedy. If you don't think prayer can help create a successful life, recall the words of former Red Cross president, Libby Dole. And if you don't think prayer gives you wisdom, consider the Dalai Lama.

Even those who pray frequently sometimes forget to pray in moments of chaos. Yet it is an effective way to the "release that leads to peace," in critical moments, especially if you remember to pray before taking the next indicated step. For the last decade I've relied on a series of prayers to change my psyche about who I am and what I deserve.

One of my favorite classic-movie lines comes from the film about Lewis Carroll's life, portrayed by Anthony

Hopkins. After a long life as a bachelor, Mr. Carroll finally falls in love and marries. Sometime later, as he leaves a chapel after his wife has been diagnosed with cancer, one of his colleagues offers condolences, and Carroll replies, "All I can do is pray. I don't pray to change God, I pray to change *me* for God."

My purpose here is not to tell you *how* to pray, but rather to urge you *to* pray. I'm going to share some of my personal prayers that I have used *to change me* for God, and you can use them, if you wish, as a guide for your own prayer work. If, in the past, you haven't found prayer fulfilling, I recommend that you give prayer another chance, until you find a method that works for you.

Prayer is a hot topic these days. *The Prayer of Jabez*, a pocketsize book by Bruce Wilkinson, dissects a short prayer from the Bible, and it's been on the *New York Times'* bestseller list. I am forever grateful to Naomi Rhode, past president of the National Speakers Association, for sharing these words and lifting my life. I've recited them so often I've converted them into my own special version. I'll give you mine first, and then the original.

> *Oh Dear God,*
> *Bless me in deed*
> *And expand my territory.*
> *Let your hand be upon me*
> *And protect me from evil*
> *That I may not cause harm to another.*

The actual prayer, from Chronicles 4:9–10, II Chapter, is as follows: "*Oh that You would bless me indeed, and enlarge my territory, that Your hand would be with me, and that You would keep me from evil, that I may not cause pain.*"

I think it's always good to go before the Creator with your own words and thoughts. After all, we are created in His image. Throughout the ages, Christian mystics and devoted spiritualists have given us beautiful words of inspiration. But sometimes we have to find our own. The shortest prayer I've ever prayed was during my father's five weeks as a quadriplegic. I was so emotionally drained after his accident that all I could say was "God help me." But it worked. Soon after, a dear friend sent me a beautiful angel cassette and video titled In Search of Angels, and its music fortified and comforted me during that critical time.

Sometimes we need special prayers for specific situations. Before I board an airplane, I always say a Christian Science prayer by Mary Baker Eddy that I learned from my mother: "Around, beneath and above are the everlasting arms of love." When I'm running late and in need of a parking space, I sometimes say, "Love makes radiant room." And the well-known Serenity Prayer is a longtime favorite; I often turn to it when my mind is racing with unresolved issues in the middle of the night or day: "God grant me the serenity to accept the things I cannot change, the courage to change the things I can, and the wisdom to know the difference."

My "quick" version of the Prayer of St. Francis almost always creates a positive difference in my attitude:

> Make me an instrument of thy peace
> That where there is hatred I may bring love,
> Darkness...Light
> Discord...Harmony.

The complete prayer is a joy to read:

Make me an instrument of thy Peace
Where there is injury let me bring pardon
Where there is doubt, faith
Where there is darkness, light
Where there is sadness, joy
O Divine Master grant that I may not so much
*   seek to be consoled*
As to console.
To be understood as to understand
To be loved as to love.
For it is in giving that we receive
It is in pardoning that we are pardoned
It is in dying to self
That we are born to Eternal Life.

Writing my own prayers has been paramount in putting my consciousness before God for transforming. The formula taught by Ernest Holmes and the teachings of Religious Science, is my favorite. I have used the following formula for years to prepare my mind for change. The benefit being, my mind gets alignment with higher wisdom and purpose.

Prayer for the Power of the Spoken Word

Seek
Align
Claim
Accept
Gratitude

Seek

I begin my prayer seeking higher wisdom and guidance. I declare the characteristics of that higher wisdom and power, and in so doing I am lifted beyond my problems.

"I recognize God as the source that operates all life. Universal unity, creator, orchestrator, and designer of all life; all-encompassing love, ever-present clarity, guidance, and wisdom are the essence of God."

Align

I now declare the characteristics of that higher wisdom and power within me and expressed in my life. From this vantage point the words I speak will have affirming power. All words have power, but these words have a strong and special intent.

"I am the Source that operates all life. I am universal unity, creator, orchestrator, and designer of all life. All-encompassing love is the essence of Me, ever-present clarity, guidance, and wisdom are the essence of Me."

Claim

I now state the solution, ideal, or goal I wish to attain. As I state my desire, I add the clause *"or better"* at the end. This is important because from my human perspective, I cannot see the big picture and don't always know what is best. (Surprise!)

"I claim that I now know the power of my spoken and written words. As I speak and write, audiences are restored to clarity, calm, and purposeful power. Well-matched clients and opportunities are continuously finding me, allowing me to act as a resource to build and renew the infrastructure of peoples' lives."

Accept

This is where I change me—my mind. I state words that release any limitations or blocks, then I claim that I am ready to accept and am able to participate in the outcome I'm praying for. This should be the longest part of the prayer because the purpose is to develop a conviction that every possible obstacle is resolved, and to build confidence that this outcome—or an even better one—is certain to occur.

"I release all my fears of deficiency. I know the power of my spoken word is divinely directed and revealing. I consciously select the words I speak and the thoughts I send out into the Universe, knowing that how I perceive life is what I experience. I perceive only the best in myself and others, therefore my life is a continual expansion, refinement, and conduit for great good. I align my consciousness with God's light and allow any self-doubt to be cleared from me and lifted into the light. I know that I am an agent of change, privileged to assist in carrying out God's plan. I release all false notions that I'm not worthy enough to carry the spoken and written word to others. I embrace all my skills and self-esteem. I embrace the fact that I chose to be an instrument for good. I release the false idea that being a powerful speaker is too demanding. I realize God is the power. I allow this power to live through me now and protect me at all times. I release all false beliefs that I'm too weak, too inconsistent, or too undisciplined to manifest a successful speaking and publishing career. Profound work is being accomplished. I align my life with God's will in an orderly direction. The voice of God is the voice in me. God is the source of my power and my message. I know that I am God's trusted instrument and I focus on aligning my life with universal good. As God's trusted instrument, I surrender any seeming blocks,

fears, and insecurities so that God's power and message can be demonstrated in my life and in the lives of the people I speak to, write for, work with, love, and cherish."

Gratitude

Here I express my gratitude for the results I am praying for. I thank my higher power as if I had already received the desired outcome.

"Thank you, wonderful God, for fulfilling my life by guiding every step of my speaking journey as a trusted orator, author, and communicator."

A book on the teachings of Rumi brought the following prayer to me. It has a special focus. Back in those days this prayer was prayed at the sighting of the crescent moon on the first day of the new year.

On the First Day of Every Year

BY AFLAKI

O Great God
You are the Eternal One
Both in the past and in the future
This is a new year
I beg You to be protected against Satan
*   and to be helped to fight against the greedy and*
*   lustful soul in me*
*   that orders me to do evil*
To busy myself with things that draw me close to you
*   and avoid those that pull me away from You*
Oh God, kind and merciful one!
I ask You this in the name of Your Pity,
Magnanimous, and All Generous One.

Use these prayers to guide and inspire you. Each of us prays in our own unique manner, and it is my hope that each of you will find your own special way of utilizing this remarkable and often miraculous power.

Sometimes it helps to have a prayer partner. My joyous prayer partner for the last twelve years gave me this little gem before an important conference I was attending. I feel such a release as I pray this and it continues to bring me great calm. I hope it does the same for you.

I recite this before I plan my day, and here is what I say:

> *Show me where to go*
> *Show me who to meet*
> *Give me the words to say*
> *and Lord keep me out of your way!*

CHAPTER THIRTEEN

Windows of Opportunity

"What lies behind us and what lies before us are tiny matters, compared to what lies within us."

—RALPH WALDO EMERSON

If we believe our lives have purpose, we can embrace the healing situations that take us to a higher plane. As I'm sure you've heard many times, we must love ourselves first before we can truly love and benefit others. All healing is derived from love, and in this state of wellness comes peace.

Long-term stress, the ultimate result of chaos, often results in depression, desperation, and demise. Chaos moves from within to without, and originates with our programmed beliefs and responses. In any given situation, what we think and how we react will either create more chaos or interject a sense of calm and control. The windows of opportunity that promote transformation often arise during times of great distress. Recognizing and responding to these "windows" can turn chaos into challenge, and challenge into victory.

Physical pain can actually be an ally. Our bodies will sometimes slip out of balance to teach us new lessons about our limitations or the importance of life balance. If we listen to our bodies, we have a chance to heal emotional baggage and stop engaging in destructive behaviors. I've found in my practice that this often occurs in people who can't seem to get the message any other way.

The following stories are about clients of mine who took advantage of a window of opportunity to free themselves from inner turmoil and tension. I feel privileged to have witnessed their healings, for each one is a small miracle.

A Woman at War with Herself

Jeanie is one of those rare women who makes her living as a professional golfer. Married with two children, she had long suffered from persistent dizziness, compounded by ear and neck problems. As I mentioned earlier, CranioSacral therapy involves removing blocks in the body, much like stones in the road. These "stones" block the body's natural ability to heal itself and remain in balance. When Jeanie came to me for treatment, I was able to provide her with some much-needed relief.

During our sessions I sensed she had a lot of tension, so I'd probe a bit and encourage her to examine the roots of her stress. In my role as healer, I've learned that the client is always right. If someone is ready to tackle a problem, I urge them to do so, but if not, I hold back. In Jeanie's case, she seemed to want to address her pain on a purely physical level, so she expended a lot of energy, time, and money seeking out specialists to diagnose her TMJ (temporomandibular joint dysfunction). But after five years all the various diagnoses hadn't helped her condition. In a last-ditch effort, she resorted to surgery because one doctor determined that her jawbone needed to be scraped in order to resolve the problem with her ear. She was pain-free for only three months, and then her symptoms returned.

Jeanie came back to me for CranioSacral therapy after a two-year absence, exclaiming angrily, "I'm so mad at myself for consenting to surgery that didn't do any good!" As we talked, I noticed that she was more anxious than ever, and she admitted to feeling "as if I'm at war with myself."

That gave me an idea. "Okay," I said, "let's visualize some kind of playing field that has a center line. Let's assume there's a separate self for every year you've been alive." Jeanie was 34 at the time, so there were 34 "Jeanies," ranging in age from one year to the present. I told her, "Now bring each 'self' onto the playing field, one by one, like players on a team. The ones who are healthy, peaceful, and confident go on one side of the field, and the ones who don't believe you deserve health, love, and compassion have to line up on the other side."

When Jeanie finished this visualization, she had four "healthy selves" and 30 "unhealthy selves." I explained what to do next. "Your job now is to heal and coax these 30 versions of yourself to join the group of happy, confident selves, so you can have a more peaceful life." Jeanie really enjoyed this investigation of herself and was finally ready to try a more spiritual approach to healing. When she did, her efforts paid off. To her amazement, her TMJ symptoms were soon relieved.

The lessons here are:

1. Each year of our lives leaves a different imprint. If we go through several years of overwhelming challenges, these "selves" formulate the belief that life is difficult, perhaps even brutal, and we often develop a "poor me" attitude.

2. Ultimately, if we are to enjoy a peaceful life, we need to discover the lessons of those years and transform them into victories, not defeats. This is how we reframe and release stored-up anxieties that result in chaos.

A Long-Delayed Farewell

Denny is another client I remember fondly. He was a strapping 40-year-old, about six-foot-three and built like a linebacker. He came in for a session because of chest and shoulder pain, assuming that an old football injury was the culprit. But as we began to work, I realized that his heart was what needed healing, for when I touched this area, memories of his father's death began to surface.

Deciding to take a risk, I asked, "Can you tell me about your father?"

Denny was silent for a moment, then said, "He had a heart attack. But we'd been estranged for years before he passed. His death happened suddenly and I wasn't there."

"Were you ever close?"

"Oh yeah, when I was a kid I loved my dad and really respected him. He was an FBI agent and he loved his work.

He'd moved up to a pretty high position and then one day he made a bad judgment call. He never forgave himself for being demoted. Instead he sort of turned inward, got depressed, and alienated the whole family—including me."

I knew that Denny had never forgiven his father, and that this was likely the source of his pain. After talking it over, we decided to create a healing ceremony so Denny could express his feelings for his father—both emotionally and verbally.

"Can you imagine that your father's here now?" I asked gently. "And is there any way you can possibly forgive him?" Denny was thoughtful for a moment, then he began to cry as he talked to his father and told him he understood how sad he must have been when he left the job, and he understood how ashamed he must have felt. It was obvious that when Denny's father lost respect for himself, he was in so much pain that he pushed everyone else out of his life. The man had never forgiven himself.

When we finished this exercise and reviewed the lessons learned, Denny's shoulder and chest pain were gone. He learned two important lessons from his father's tragedy:

1. Never identify so intensely with a job that you lose yourself.

2. No matter what mistakes you make in life, find a way to forgive yourself and move on.

Healing a Childhood Trauma

Marcy was 62 when she came in for her first session. She was in the midst of a career change and her coaches were having a difficult time. She was not receptive to their ideas and was struggling to find the right direction. As I began to work with her, it seemed that both her heart and her throat were calling out for attention. As I received these strong responses from her body, I asked, "Right now, what's going on in your mind?" Even as I spoke, the pulsing energy was so strong in her chest that I knew some powerful emotions needed to be freed up.

Marcy told me she was recalling an incident from her childhood. "When I was a kid," she said, "we lived on a farm in Oklahoma, really out in the boonies. Our rare trips to town took over an hour. One day when we were at the country store, I saw this beautiful, shiny cash register and I begged my father to buy it for me."

"A cash register?"

Marcy smiled. "Unlikely toy, huh? But at the ripe old age of six, I wanted to start a business—you know, a play store. My dad said it was too expensive. But I was so motivated that I started saving money, doing odd jobs and stuff, and a month later I actually had enough to buy it. When the long-awaited day arrived, my parents took me back into town, but the cash register was gone."

I could feel the tension in Marcy's body as she spoke. "You must have been crushed."

"I was nearly hysterical the whole way home. But my father didn't understand, he didn't apologize or try to work something out so I could get another one. All I could do was cry."

That cash register had meant everything to this little girl, and her parents had no idea how devastated she was. As a result, Marcy put a shield around her heart, effectively saying, "No matter how hard you work, nobody cares." As she recounted a number of situations that had gone wrong in her life, I realized this theme had played out in her marriages and business endeavors.

To heal Marcy's hardened heart, I asked her to relive that long-ago scene when she was six. The difference was that now, as an adult, she would intervene and tell the little girl that people *do* care, and that she was a very ingenious child. As this scenario transpired, the shield slipped off, all rusted out like a junked car. At the same time, the block in the heart and throat of Marcy—the child—was released, and simultaneously, Marcy—the woman—was healed.

After her session, Marcy began to move in the direction of her dreams, and was more open to suggestions and encouragement. Her coaches even called to tell me that something very positive had occurred, that Marcy had begun looking and acting more youthful and alive.

The lessons here are:

1. What you think about comes about.

2. If you want to improve your life take actions to improve your thinking.

A Legacy of Pain

Sometimes blocks are passed down from our parents and even our forefathers. Doris was a client who had incredible anger for her father, because she felt he had stifled her desire to become a graphic artist. He'd urged her to follow the course expected of women in those days—either nursing or teaching—so she had become a nurse. When we began our first session, Doris had a major block in her throat. It almost looked like something was hooked around it. When I described this to her, she asked, "Could it have anything to do with my grandfather hanging himself in jail?"

I was taken aback for a moment, then said, "Very possibly. Tell me what happened."

Doris looked grim. "The way I heard it, my grandfather was jailed one night, for being drunk in public. He was a respectable man, and in his state of drunkenness and despair, I guess he decided to end his life. This tragedy, of course, changed my dad's life, and he ended up in a foster home when he was only seven. The shame from this obviously left him very repressed. His intellect was his saving grace; he became a college professor, but he was never able to express emotions of love to my mother or me."

I recognized this as a multigenerational block. This example is important in teaching us how patterns and secrets can sometimes be passed down from parents or even grandparents. When we keep these traumas repressed, they block our life force, which reflects in our health and well-being.

There's an expression: "You're as sick as your secrets," and I think it's often literally true. This is why so many lives are forever changed during this life-exploration process. In Doris's case, because of the lack of love in her parents' marriage, she had remained single. After going through several sessions to reframe these experiences, this intuitive nurse and healer realized that part of her life's purpose was to heal her family's pattern of unexpressed emotions.

Once she began making progress, Doris gained confidence and was determined to start a new career and open herself up to romance. The day we finished our work she smiled at me and said, "I don't think I need to see you anymore." I happily concurred and she went on her way. Several lessons came out of this session:

1. We aren't always the cause of our unresolved emotional issues, they get passed on.
2. Never give up looking for a way to clear yourself of this baggage that blocks the good things in life.
3. All major life events teach us incredible lessons if we remain teachable.

A New Window for All of Us

Facing up to vulnerabilities, loss, addiction, and catastrophe ultimately makes us stronger—if we embrace and face our difficult times. Life moments are real, life achievements are real, materialism is not. Our unprecedented affluence during the '90s caused many of us to veer away from our real values.

If you've let friendships slide in your pursuit of success and you suffer a loss, to whom do you turn? Even if you have an abundance of acquaintances, the challenges we face in the 24/7 society seem more complex. What is your solace? Accepting some form of Higher Power or Benevolent Providence can be a great source of comfort and calm. Reflecting on some of the suggestions in this book will also help bring you back to the basics of life.

When life delivers events that turn us upside down, we need to pray for strength and a new sense of direction. When our friends are hit with tragedy it may stir up our own past traumas that have never been healed. It is during these times we need to heal the losses we've endured—neglected friendships, lost opportunities, and abandoned dreams. Once we fully acknowledge these hurts, we can proceed to heal them and they often disappear. This is the way to clear the slate: Tally up your life experiences and move forward, tackling new challenges from a position of strength.

Many people are searching for meaning in their lives. They feel they aren't valued or their values don't matter, so why bother? Values are the backbone of who you are. What you value matters.

The paramount solution in finding calm in this unsettled world is knowing what you value and living accordingly. Sometimes we "think" we know what we value or who we are, yet we haven't taken time to investigate ourselves to really find out. Thinking and knowing are two different things. The knower is calm and content, the thinker is chaotic and uncertain.

My beloved teacher Ken Sutherland used to tell me as he'd point to his heart, "All the answers are here." Then he'd point to his head and say, "Not here." At the time I thought the thinking mind was all-powerful and the ultimate solution-finder. Today I know better. And knowing is calming.

Your answers to finding your calm are as unique as you. For those who are seeking to know their values and inner fortitude, as we share our stories and experiences, we light the way for one another.

Each obstacle in your life is a window of opportunity to grow you into greater knowing. If we embrace our trials with this kind of faith, and extend it to each person who crosses our path, it is the first step toward peace in our hearts—and peace in the world.

We Want to Hear From YOU

As you make positive steps to a calmer life, we want to hear about your success! Please write and tell us: Include a brief outline of what the circumstance or challenge was, what steps you took to change, and how you transformed from Chaos to Calm. Each year we select ten top stories. If you are selected, we will send you a complimentary audio tape set. We also ask you for the rights to publish your story in upcoming books and articles to encourage others.

Send your good news to:

Creative Living Publications
306 NW El Norte Pkwy, #426
Escondido, CA 92026

Attn: Success Stories

Healthcare Resources

Alexander Technique

The Alexander Technique International's website (www.ati-net.com) will help you locate a trained instructor. You may contact the main office in the U.S. at 1692 Massachusetts Avenue, 3rd Floor, Cambridge, MA 02138 or 1-888-668-8996.

CranioSacral Therapy

For more information on obtaining a CranioSacral Therapist call the Upledger Institute at 1-800-233-5880, or write 11211 Prosperity Farms Road, D-325, Palm Beach Gardens, FL 33410-3487. Or contact the International Alliance of Healthcare Educators at their website www. iahe.com.

Essential Oils

For blended oils I recommend a company out of Salt Lake City, distributed through multilevel marketing. These blends are nothing short of miraculous. If you'd like to sample the wizardry of Young Living Essential Oils, you may call 1-800-763-9963 to place an order. Here are the oils I recommend for stress-related conditions. When they ask for your sponsor number, enter 79014, then proceed by using the code numbers listed below. After your first order arrives you will receive a price list with additional oils and products.

Name of Oil	Code No.	Price	Amt.	Assists With
Acceptance	3303	$30.00	5 ml.	Security, Understanding
Brain Power	3313	36.00	5 ml.	Enthusiasm, Concentration
Joy	3372	28.00	15 ml.	Confidence, Happiness
Peace & Calming	3393	18.00	15 ml.	Stability, Focus
Valor	3429	18.00	15 ml.	Growth, Peace
White Angelica	3432	38.00	15 ml.	Balance, Connectedness

The real gift in using these oils is knowing where to apply them for maximum benefit. The best resource I have found is the book *Releasing Emotional Patterns with Essential Oils* by Carolyn Mein, D.C. You may order it for $15.00, plus shipping, at www.bodytype.com or 1-858-756-3704.

Essential Oils: Body Care

One of the best "feel good" stores around is Origins. In stores you are encouraged to sample the various creams, bath gels, and salt scrubs. Just visiting a store is relaxing in itself. Recommended products are Peace of Mind on the Spot gel, Ginger Body Scrub and Salt Rub, Clean Comfort and Salt Suds bath gels, Ginger Soufflé body cream, and Ginger Burst body wash. See Chapter 11 for more information. To purchase call Origins at 1-800-ORIGINS (1-800-674-4467) or visit their website at www.origins.com for the store nearest you.

Home Fragrance and Incense

For home fragrances, contact Thymes Limited, out of Minneapolis. Their number and website are 800-366-4071 and www.thymes.com. A few of my favorites are Green Tea, Eucalyptus, and Lavender. These fragrances cost a little more but are very clean, refreshing, and long lasting. For those who enjoy a pure-smelling incense, one of my favorite companies is Escential Essences at www.matchlessgifts.com. A few of my favorites are Purification, Prosperity, and Energy.

Lymph Drainage Therapy

To locate a Lymph Drainage Therapist, or purchase Dr. Bruno Chikly's book, *Silent Waves, Theory and Practice of Lymph Drainage Therapy*, contact International Alliance of Healthcare Educators (IAHE) at 800-233-5880.

Massage and Healing Techniques

A good resource for additional massage and healing techniques is the book *Alternative Healing* by Mark Kastner, L.Ac., and Hugh Burroughs, which provides an A–Z guide to alternative therapies.

Personal Rejuvenizers

Personal Rejuvenizers help restore the body by pro-tecting against Electromagnetic Fields (EMFs). If you work on the computer all day, are surrounded by office equip-ment, and experience fatigue and eyestrain, you could be sensitive to EMFs. This product harmonizes your physical and subtle energy fields, strengthening the immunity and creating a sense of well-being and vitality. Besides being good for your health they are also beautiful. (If you'd like to view an assortment, visit www.creativelifesolutions and have a look.) The cost is $135 plus shipping and handling with a 30-day money-back guarantee.

Sea Salts

Using mineral and dead sea salts is a wonderful rem-edy for people with insomnia. A salt soak before bed leads to restful sleep because it purifies and relaxes. BathTherapy and Masada Dead Sea Salts are available at most health food stores. For high-powered bathers, I recommend Kerstin Florian Mineral Kur bath salts. If you are getting a cold, these salts boost the immune system. For informa-tion on where to purchase these mineral salts and creams call 510-549-8566 or 800-232-9098.

Give the Gift of
Staying Calm in the Midst of Chaos™

❑ YES, I want _____ copies of *Staying Calm in the Midst of Chaos*™ at $14.95 each (book)

❑ YES, I want _____ copies of *Burnout to Brilliance: Self Care and Soul Care for Life Repair* at $45.00 per set (three cassette audio album includes meditation tape)

❑ YES, I want _____ copies of the Complete Package at $55.00 (one book and one tape set)

Add $4.95 shipping first item; $1.95 each additional item.
(California residents please add 7.75% sales tax.) Canadian orders
must be accompanied by a postal money order in U.S. funds.
Quantity discounts available on book orders. Allow 15 days for delivery.

Choose one of the following to order:

1. Call us toll free 1-866-246-0462 with your credit card information.
2. Copy this form and fax it with your credit card number to 760-741-3933.
3. E-mail us at CGrossCLS@aol.com with your credit card information.
4. Copy this order form and mail it with your check or credit card number to:

Creative Living Publications
306 NW El Norte Parkway, #426; Escondido, CA 92026
· ·

My check or money order for $_____ is enclosed.
Please charge my: ❑ Visa   ❑ MasterCard
                    ❑ Discover   ❑ American Express

Name _____

Organization _____

Address _____

City/State/Zip _____

Phone_____ E-mail _____

Card # _____

Exp. Date_____ Signature _____

website
light unlimited. com
stores

Nov. 2005

CGross. com
CarolynGross. com